BREAD,
CAKE,
DOUGHNUT,
PUDDING

Published by the Penguin Group

Penguin Books Ltd, 80 Strand, London WC2R 0RL, England

Penguin Group (USA) Inc., 375 Hudson Street, New York, New York 10014, USA

Penguin Group (Canada), 90 Eglinton Avenue East, Suite 700, Toronto, Ontario, Canada M4P 2Y3

(a division of Pearson Penguin Canada Inc.)

Penguin Ireland, 25 St Stephen's Green, Dublin 2, Ireland (a division of Penguin Books Ltd)

Penguin Group (Australia), 707 Collins Street, Melbourne,

Victoria 3008, Australia (a division of Pearson Australia Group Pty Ltd)

Penguin Books India Pvt Ltd, 11 Community Centre,

Panchsheel Park, New Delhi – 110 017, India

Penguin Group (NZ), 67 Apollo Drive, Rosedale, Auckland 0632, New Zealand

(a division of Pearson New Zealand Ltd)

Penguin Books (South Africa) (Pty) Ltd, Block D, Rosebank Office Park,

181 Jan Smuts Avenue, Parktown North, Gauteng 2193, South Africa

Penguin Books Ltd, Registered Offices: 80 Strand, London WC2R 0RL, England

www.penguin.com

First published 2014

001

Copyright © Justin Gellatly, 2014

Photography copyright © Andy Sewell, 2014

The moral right of the author has been asserted

Designed by Nathan Burton

Set in Gill Sans

Printed in China

A CIP catalogue record for this book is available from the British Library

ISBN: 978–0–241–14605–7

www.greenpenguin.co.uk

Penguin Books is committed to a sustainable
future for our business, our readers and
our planet. This book is made from Forest
Stewardship Council™ certified paper.

MIX
Paper from
responsible sources
FSC
www.fsc.org   FSC™ C018179

BREAD, CAKE, DOUGHNUT, PUDDING

Sweet and Savoury Recipes
from Britain's Best Baker

JUSTIN GELLATLY

PHOTOGRAPHY BY
ANDY SEWELL

FIG TREE
an imprint of
PENGUIN BOOKS

For my wonderful wife, Louise

And for
Fergus Henderson and Trevor Gulliver for everything

CONTENTS

INTRODUCTION

Baking has always been part of my life. My mother used to bake bread most days when we were children, and even at my first job at Crowthers, a family-run restaurant in East Sheen, London, where I began by washing dishes, I would help to bake the bread until I moved on to do cooking and pastry.

I met my wife, Louise, when I was sixteen at Hounslow catering college. We were in the same class, and one of the many reasons we are still happy together after twenty-four years is that we both understand the demands of a life as a chef or baker.

After Crowthers I worked in many other restaurants: in Cheshire at the Rookery Hall, in Maine, USA, where I cooked up a storm on Little Cranberry Island, and at the Greenhouse in Mayfair, London, to name but a few.

But it was only when I joined Fergus Henderson at St John Restaurant that I really fell in love with baking. Even in my early days as a chef, I always liked cooking 'nose to tail', so when an opportunity came along to work at St John I dived in. Those were the most amazing thirteen years: I found my calling in pastry and baking in the first few months.

One of the turning points was when I did my first bake at St John and took my first loaf of bread out of the oven. The bread and the crackling of the crust just didn't stop singing to me. I hung up my chef apron and put on a baker's one, and never looked back.

I owe Fergus Henderson and his partner and co-founder of St John, Trevor Gulliver, so much. There were many joyous occasions at St John, but one of my proudest was receiving our first Michelin star when I was Head Baker and Pastry Chef.

A few months after leaving St John, a fellow baker, Matt Jones, called me and told me he had found a site for a bakery in Borough Market and asked whether I would be interested in coming on board. I said 'hell, yeah' and we opened Bread Ahead in the summer of 2013.

Bread Ahead stands for British baking; we bake our bread using British wheat but use lots of sourdough and long fermentation. We bake early in the morning and throughout the day (so no more night shifts) and we have large windows at the front of the bakery so people can come and watch us working our magic, but also we get to see daylight – happy days.

We are opening a bakery school alongside the bakery, teaching people how to make bread, cakes and, of course, doughnuts – but I hope that you can learn the ropes through experimenting with the recipes in this book.

I have worked in every section in a kitchen, from kitchen porter to head chef, and I've found the baker's life the hardest – but it's a passion and I love it, and it's become a way of life.

THOSE DOUGHNUTS

A baker's life isn't all bread. I started making my doughnuts in 2003 when St John Bread & Wine opened, but I had many teething issues with getting the recipe right, from the sweetness of the dough to the length of the proving and cooking times, and even the yeast amounts. Yes, we did have exploding doughnuts. After many trials, I got there, and I think they are perfect. I've made them for a prestigious lunch for the world's fifty best restaurants and I even took my fryer to Glastonbury in 2013 where I rocked at the Beat Hotel, frying doughnuts until the early morning, and launched my violet custard doughnut with sugared violets and Parma violet sprinkle. So turn to page 143 and you can enjoy all my hard work and make the perfect doughnuts too.

BEFORE YOU BEGIN

Every recipe in this book has been carefully tested and timed, so you can easily see at a glance how much time you will need to prepare and make or bake it. If you want to make my sourdough, for example, you will need to start your mother a week in advance.

It may sound like obvious advice, but read through the recipe carefully before you begin. It's important to make sure you have all the necessary ingredients and the right equipment (baking is an exact science, and even if you follow a recipe exactly, if you use a 28cm cake tin when the recipe has been designed for a 23cm tin, then you are not going to get the right results).

Finally, quite a few of the recipes in the book call for things from the Store Cupboard chapter on page 239, whether it's jam, chocolate sauce or butterscotch, so check what you need before you begin and stock up your cupboard.

BREAKFAST

They say breakfast is the most important meal of the day, but, as a baker, when most people are having their breakfast I am usually tucking into my dinner with a glass of wine.

Breakfast happens at very different times: when working through the night, breakfast could be at 10 p.m. (that's when William's spud fry is perfect), but most of the time it's bread or toast or granola – the clusters are brilliant for when you're on the go, as are the flapjack bars.

If you ever need to score a few brownie points, pull out the full Monty soufflés and serve them in bed with some bubbles.

I also love to go out for breakfast at good restaurants in town (London), like Quo Vadis, One Leicester Street, Smiths of Smithfield and, for the best bacon sandwich, St John Bread & Wine – you get to have a bit of glamour without breaking the bank.

BREAKFAST BUN SCROLLS

I developed these buns for the St John Hotel breakfast menu, as we wanted something different from the normal pastry offerings. These amazing buns are a cross between the softest buttery bun and pastry.

Put the flour and salt into a bowl and mix together. Whisk the yeast into the milk, then add to the flour and mix together for only a couple of minutes. Scrape out of the bowl on to a lightly floured surface and form into a ball, then wrap it in clingfilm and put into the fridge for 2 hours to rest.

Take the butter out of the fridge, followed about 15 minutes later by the dough. Let them both come to room temperature (they need to be the same).

On a lightly floured surface, start rolling the dough lengthways until you have a long, even, rectangular strip about 70cm long and 24cm wide. Brush off any excess flour and make sure all the sides and corners are straight and even.

With one of the shorter sides of the rectangle facing you, place the butter in small knobs evenly all over the top two-thirds of the dough. Fold the bottom (unbuttered) third into the middle, then flip the folded two-thirds on to the buttered third to cover it. This is your first turn.

Turn the dough so that the seam or join is always on the right, then roll it out again and fold just as before. This is your second turn.

Wrap the dough in clingfilm and put it back into the fridge to rest for another 2 hours, then repeat another two turns, again resting for 2 hours.

Now make the last turn by rolling the dough out to the same size but folding in the top to the middle and the bottom to the middle (so that it looks like an open book). Fold it in half so that now the book is closed, then again wrap in clingfilm and leave for 2 hours or overnight in the fridge.

Lightly oil and flour two 12-hole muffin tins. Cut the dough in half and roll out 2 rectangles about 1cm thick, 30cm long and 20cm wide. Roll each one up tightly lengthways, then brush the end with eggwash to seal it and slice into 3cm thick scrolls. You should have about 20.

Pop the scrolls cut side up in the prepared tins. Cover loosely with clingfilm and leave to prove for 2 hours somewhere warm, until they have doubled in size.

Preheat the oven to 180°C/fan 160°C/gas 4. Eggwash the tops of the scrolls and bake for 15–20 minutes, until golden brown.

Serve warm, with butter and jam.

»

Makes about 20
Suitable for freezing (cooked, or rolled raw, or sliced)
Preparation time: 50 minutes
Proving/resting time: 8 hours and/or overnight
Cooking time: 20 minutes

500g strong white bread flour, plus extra for dusting
10g fine sea salt
10g fresh yeast, crumbled
350ml full fat milk
250g unsalted butter
1 egg, beaten, to glaze

You can spice up the breakfast buns by using a spiced butter:
add 3 teaspoons of ground cinnamon, 1 teaspoon of ground nutmeg,
1 teaspoon of ground cloves, 1 teaspoon of ground mace,
1 teaspoon of ground ginger and 35g of demerara sugar to
the butter and mix together.

You can also add dried fruit: soak 25g of currants,
25g of raisins and 25g of sultanas in 250ml of water overnight, then
squeeze out the excess water and mix into the butter with the zest
of 1 orange and 1 tablespoon of caster sugar.

All the buns are nice with a sugary glaze (see below).

**All are good served warm, either on their own or with butter,
honey or jam.**

SUGAR GLAZE

Put all the ingredients into a heavy-based saucepan. Bring to the boil,
then reduce the heat and simmer until the mixture reaches 105°C
on a kitchen thermometer. Leave to cool. When the buns are cooked,
brush them with the glaze while they are still warm.

100g sugar
100g water
20g liquid glucose

OLD-FASHIONED ENGLISH MUFFINS

Pour the milk into a jug and whisk in the yeast until dissolved. Whisk in the sugar and leave to stand for 10 minutes.

Put the flour, salt and butter into a large bowl and rub together with your fingertips until you have fine crumbs. Stir in the milk mixture, then transfer to a lightly floured work surface and knead briefly until a smooth dough is formed. You can do this by hand or using an electric mixer with a dough hook.

Cover the bowl lightly with clingfilm and leave somewhere warm to prove for 2 hours.

Line a baking tray (24cm x 34cm) with baking paper. On a lightly floured surface, roll out the dough to 2cm thick. Then, using a 7cm round cutter, cut out 6–8 rounds and roll out the trimmings to get 2 more. Place them on the prepared baking tray, cover, and leave for 45 minutes to 1 hour, until doubled in size.

Preheat the oven to 180°C/fan 160°C/gas 4. Bake the muffins for 5 minutes, then turn them over and bake for a further 5 minutes, until lightly golden brown. Place on a rack and leave to cool.

To serve, cut the muffins open and toast them. Serve warm, with lashings of butter or the old favourites – ham, poached egg and hollandaise.

Makes 8 – 10
Suitable for freezing
Preparation time: 20 minutes
Proving/resting time: 3 hours
Cooking time: 12 minutes

225ml full fat milk
20g fresh yeast, crumbled
1 teaspoon caster sugar
450g plain flour, plus extra
   for dusting
1 teaspoon fine sea salt
75g cold lard or butter, diced

PIKELETS

Originally from the West Midlands, these are like a flat crumpet but a little heavier (and you don't need crumpet rings).

Warm the milk and sugar together in a medium saucepan until just warm (blood heat), then whisk in the yeast until dissolved.

Sift the flours into a large bowl and add the salt, the milk mixture and 1 tablespoon of sunflower oil. Whisk together until you have a smooth, thick batter mixture. Cover loosely with a cloth or clingfilm and leave somewhere warm to prove for 1 hour, or until doubled in size.

You will need to cook the pikelets in three batches. Pour 2 tablespoons of oil into a large, heavy-based frying pan on a medium heat. When hot, pour in 3–4 separate ladlefuls of batter, leaving a little space between them as they spread out when cooking. Turn the heat right down and fry for 3 minutes on each side, until golden brown.

Remove the pikelets from the oil with a spatula and place them on kitchen paper to drain. Continue with the remaining two batches, using more oil as necessary.

Serve warm, with butter and jam or honey.

Makes 10 – 12
Suitable for freezing
Preparation time: 15 minutes
Proving/resting time: 1 hour
Cooking time: 20 minutes

360ml full fat milk
½ teaspoon caster sugar
14g fresh yeast, crumbled
125g strong white bread flour
125g plain flour
1½ teaspoons fine sea salt
3–5 tablespoons sunflower oil

BREAKFAST PANCAKES

These light American style pancakes are really simple to knock up any time – not just for breakfast.

Sift the flour, baking powder and salt into a large bowl and stir in the sugar. In a jug, whisk together the milk, melted butter and egg until combined, then pour into the dry ingredients and mix well, using a whisk, until the mixture is smooth.

Cook the pancakes in batches. Heat a large non-stick frying pan to a medium to high heat. Drizzle a little oil into the pan, then ladle in about 3 tablespoons of the mixture and cook for 1–1½ minutes on each side.

Serve with your bacon and eggs, or just with a squeeze of lemon or a drizzle of maple syrup...or with fresh fruit.

Makes about 12 (3 per person)
Suitable for freezing
Preparation time: 10 minutes
Cooking time: 8 minutes

150g plain flour
3 teaspoons baking powder
½ teaspoon fine sea salt
20g caster sugar
250ml full fat milk
25g unsalted butter, melted
1 egg
sunflower oil, for cooking

GRAPE NUTS

There are no grapes or nuts in this recipe, but after they are broken up they sort of look like grape seeds/nuts – though there are a few other stories... As well as having them for breakfast you can fold them through vanilla ice cream or use them as a sprinkle. If you can't get hold of buttermilk, use natural yoghurt instead.

Makes 500g
Not suitable for freezing
Preparation time: 15 minutes
Cooking time: 50–55 minutes

Preheat the oven to 160°C/fan 140°C/gas 3 and line two large baking trays (approximately 38cm x 28cm) with baking paper.

Mix the flour, sugar, salt and bicarbonate of soda in a large bowl, then stir in the buttermilk. Put into a piping bag with no nozzle, or a disposable one cut to 4cm, and pipe out four rows measuring about 38cm lengthways on each prepared tray, leaving room between them so that they can spread out. Pat them down slightly with a wet finger so that they are about 1cm high.

Bake for 20 minutes, until golden brown, then cool on a rack. Once cool, break up into small pieces (nuts) – they will still be a bit soft – then put them back on the lined baking tray and bake for another 30–35 minutes, stirring a few times so they brown evenly – they should turn a dark golden brown and be crisp in places. Leave on the tray to cool and they will crisp up further.

When cool, store in an airtight container, where they will keep for 2 months. Serve with a jug of cold milk or use the nuts as a sprinkle for creamy desserts like buttermilk pudding (see page 194).

360g Maltstar bread flour
150g light brown sugar
1 teaspoon fine sea salt
5g bicarbonate of soda
300ml buttermilk

GRANOLA CLUSTERS

These are the most delicious buttery crunchy clusters, great for breakfast or as a snack.

Preheat the oven to 140°C/fan 120°C/gas 1 and line two large baking trays (approximately 38cm x 28cm) with baking paper.

Roughly chop the hazelnuts and put them into a large bowl with the oats, salt, sunflower and pumpkin seeds.

Put the butter, honey, golden syrup and all the sugars into a saucepan and melt everything together over a low heat, stirring constantly. Once melted, pour into the bowl of oats and stir until all the dry ingredients are coated in the melted butter mix.

Spread the mixture thinly and evenly over the prepared baking trays, then bake for about 45 minutes, until golden brown. Note: do not stir the mix at all.

Once cooked, leave until cool enough to handle, then break up into clusters. Store in an airtight container for up to a month.

Serve with yoghurt and fresh fruit, or just munch as a snack.

Makes 1.1kg
Not suitable for freezing
Preparation time: 15 minutes
Cooking time: 45 minutes

160g whole peeled hazelnuts
   (or any other nut you fancy)
375g jumbo oats
3g fine sea salt
70g sunflower seeds
70g pumpkin seeds
130g butter
150g clear honey
50g golden syrup
75g caster sugar
125g soft light brown sugar
40g demerara sugar

FRUIT GRANOLA

Preheat the oven to 180°C/fan 160°C/gas 4, and line two large baking trays (approximately 38cm x 28cm) with baking paper.

Roughly chop the almonds and put them into a large bowl with the oats and salt.

Split the vanilla pod lengthways and scrape out the seeds. Put both pod and seeds into a saucepan with the butter and honey. Melt together over a low heat, stirring, then remove and discard the vanilla pod. Pour the mixture into the bowl of oats and nuts and mix well together, then spread evenly over the prepared baking trays and bake for 30 minutes, until golden brown, stirring every 5 minutes so you get evenly toasted oats.

Once baked and golden brown, remove from the oven and leave to cool completely.

Slice the dried apricots finely and add to the cooled oat mix with the rest of the dried fruit. Mix well, and store in an airtight container.

Serve with yoghurt and a drizzle of honey.

Makes 2.5kg
Not suitable for freezing
Preparation time: 15 minutes
Cooking time: 30 minutes

260g whole, skin-on almonds
1kg jumbo oats
a pinch of fine sea salt
1 vanilla pod
250g unsalted butter,
    cut into large cubes
250g clear honey
300g dried, ready-to-eat apricots
250g raisins
200g dried cranberries
100g currants

FLAPJACK BREAKFAST BARS

These are great for when you're on the go.

Preheat the oven to 180°C/fan 160°C/gas 4 and line a baking tray (24cm x 34cm x 2cm) with baking paper.

Put the oats and salt into a large bowl.

Put the butter, golden syrup and light brown sugar into a heavy-based saucepan and melt together over a low heat, stirring constantly. Once melted, pour into the bowl of oats and stir together, making sure all the oats are coated in the butter mix. Stir in the prunes and almonds.

Spread evenly over the prepared baking tray and press down firmly, then bake for 20 minutes, until golden brown.

Leave to cool for a couple of hours, marking into squares, big or small, after 30 minutes, and just before it gets completely cold, cut into your desired pieces.

Makes about 12 large squares
or 24 small ones
Not suitable for freezing
Preparation time: 10 minutes
Cooking time: 20 minutes

300g jumbo oats
a pinch of fine sea salt
165g butter, cut into big cubes
100g golden syrup
100g soft light brown sugar
180g stoned chopped prunes
50g chopped whole almonds

WILLIAM'S SPUD FRY

This recipe was inspired by my father, William Neil Gellatly. By all accounts he came up with it when he was serving in the Royal Household Cavalry; he used to make it often for us as kids, and served it with all sorts.

Serves 4
Not suitable for freezing
Preparation time: 10 minutes
Resting time: 10 minutes
Cooking time: 35 minutes

Preheat the oven to 200°C/fan 180°C/gas 6.

Coarsely grate the potatoes, leaving the skins on, then put them into a large bowl and sprinkle them with about 1 teaspoon of salt. Mix well, then leave to stand for 10 minutes.

Peel and dice the onions and crush the garlic. Put the butter and oil into a large non-stick ovenproof frying pan over a medium heat. Add the onions, garlic, bay leaf and thyme sprigs and cook for about 15 minutes, until the onions and garlic are soft.

Squeeze out the potatoes a handful at a time and put them into another bowl, discarding the liquid. Season them with ground white pepper and a small pinch of salt. Remove the thyme and bay leaf from the frying pan and discard, then add the potato mixture to the pan and mix well, pressing the mixture down with the back of a spoon.

Drizzle a little more oil around the outside of the potatoes and cook for 5 minutes on a low to medium heat, then transfer to the oven and bake for 10 – 15 minutes, until golden brown and crispy and the potatoes are cooked through.

750g large potatoes (e.g. Maris Piper)
salt and ground white pepper
2 large Spanish onions
4 cloves of garlic
a large knob of butter
2 tablespoons olive oil
1 bay leaf
4 sprigs of fresh thyme

To serve, check out the following alternatives:

1. With 2 eggs per person, cooked any way.

2. Cover with melted cheese and put under the grill, then add a few splashes of Worcestershire sauce.

3. As a topping for mince.

4. With chopped hard-boiled eggs, crispy bacon and chopped parsley.

5. As part of a full English breakfast.

6. On its own, with plum ketchup (see page 255).

7. With smoked kippers.

8. With smoked salmon and scrambled eggs.

THE FULL MONTY SOUFFLÉ

This is a great breakfast to serve in bed for a special occasion, and beats a croissant any day. You can make it the day before, up to the point where it's ready to put into the oven, which is good, as otherwise it's quite a bit of work first thing in the morning. It's also a good way of glamming up any breakfast leftovers: just make the soufflé mix and fold in the leftovers.

Makes 4 individual soufflés
Not suitable for freezing
Preparation time: 30 minutes
Cooking time: 50 minutes

Preheat the oven to 180°C/fan 160°C/gas 4. Whiz the bread to fine crumbs in a food processor (you will need 150g of crumbs), then put them on a baking tray and toast them in the oven until crisp and golden brown. Set aside to cool.

Turn the oven up to 200°C/fan 180°C/gas 6 and put a baking sheet on the top shelf to get hot.

Melt 5g of the butter and lightly brush over the inside of four 200ml ramekins. Put some of the cooled breadcrumbs into each ramekin and turn them until all the inside is covered (tip out any excess).

Heat the oil in a large frying pan, add the sausages, and cook for 15–20 minutes, turning regularly. Add the black pudding and bacon about halfway through, and the mushrooms and sun-dried tomatoes for the final 5 minutes. Leave to cool, then cut everything into bite-size pieces.

Meanwhile, melt the remaining butter in a medium saucepan. Add the sifted flour and cook on a low heat for 2 minutes, then slowly add the milk, whisking all the time, bringing it to the boil after each addition. Reduce to a light simmer for 2 minutes, then take off the heat, add the mustard and season well.

Cool slightly, then stir in the grated cheese. Add the beaten egg yolks, one at a time, and once all is incorporated pour into a large bowl.

In a separate metal or glass bowl, whisk the egg whites to the soft peaks stage. Spoon the whites into the bowl of sauce and fold together. When the whites are nearly incorporated, add the cooked ingredients and finish folding in.

Gently divide your mix between your prepared ramekins, making sure everyone gets a share of the cooked ingredients. Place on the hot baking tray and bake for 20 minutes, until risen and golden brown.

Serve with red or brown sauce, or plum ketchup (see page 255).

2 thick slices of white bread, crusts removed
25g butter
1 tablespoon sunflower or rapeseed oil
4 chipolata sausages
4 slices of black pudding
4 rashers of smoked bacon
4 button mushrooms
8 sun-dried tomatoes
20g plain flour, sifted
150ml full fat milk
¼ teaspoon English mustard
fine sea salt and ground white pepper
50g Cornish Yarg or Cheddar cheese, grated
2 eggs, separated

BAKING
AND BREAD

I have tried to make my baking recipes simple for the home baker, as I know how hard it can seem to make good bread at home. When I'm working, I am used to using commercial ovens with steam injection and top and bottom heat, and mixers which can do so much. But I assure you that I have made all these recipes at home and they work!

With the bread recipes I always use fresh yeast, crumbled up and dissolved in water, but if using dried, use half the yeast amount in the recipe. I also always use a good fine sea salt and cold water from the tap.

I always weigh the water when making bread; it's a lot more accurate than using a measuring jug. So digital scales are a must.

Also, I always use large eggs.

Baking is not just about bread – there are many other recipes included in this chapter (give the madeleines a try as well). With baking, the recipes can work but sometimes, with the weather, heat and even if you are just in a bad mood, things will change, so remember that practice makes perfect. Be confident with your baking and you will wonder why you didn't start sooner.

I tend to use an electric mixer because I am normally baking and making several things at once in the kitchen, and using a mixer keeps your hands free to do other things.

But you can make all of these breads and cakes by hand, by following these simple steps:

1. Prepare your yeast and water as the recipe states.

2. Put your dry ingredients in a bowl.

3. Follow recipe.

4. Mix by hand until all incorporated.

5. Turn out on to a floured surface and knead until elastic and smooth or as the recipe has stated.

Essential kit for baking:

1. A mixer.

2. A dough scraper.

3. Plastic bowls – a range of sizes.

4. A proving basket (this holds the shape of your bread as it proves).

5. Digital scales.

6. Clingfilm.

7. Baking trays – a range of sizes.

8. Loaf tins – a range of sizes.

9. Baking paper.

10. A sieve.

11. A pastry brush.

12. A heavy-based saucepan.

STARTERS

The main bread recipes (apart from soda bread) use three different types of starter:

FERMENT (page 36, and see also Savoury Baking, pages 77 and 80)

OLD DOUGH (page 50)

SOURDOUGH (page 53)

Using ferment and old dough is a way to enhance the flavour and texture of your bread. It's really just flour, water and a small amount of yeast that, left for 24 hours, will start fermentation, which helps to create greater depth of flavour.

Sourdough is the best way to make bread, with a culture of stable natural yeast that you feed and look after. It's worth the time, as the results are really good and you are left with an amazing depth of flavour and the best crusts – really nice and chewy. I know the sourdough starter is a bit of work, but once it is up and running it becomes part of the family.

BLINIS

The perfect nibbles for canapés or a starter. Try the following as toppings: smoked salmon and soured cream, rare roast beef and horseradish, cream cheese and chives, grilled mackerel and pickled beetroot, strong Cheddar and piccalilli ... or make up your own combinations.

Makes about 24 large blinis
   or 48 canapé size
Suitable for freezing
Preparation time: 10 minutes
Proving/resting time: 1½ hours
Cooking time: 20 minutes

250ml full fat milk
7g fresh yeast, crumbled
3 eggs, separated
100g strong white bread flour
100g wholegrain buckwheat flour
10g caster sugar
6g fine sea salt
about 50g butter
3–4 tablespoons oil

Warm the milk slightly in a small pan, then whisk in the yeast and egg yolks and leave to one side for 15 minutes.

Sift the flours into a large bowl and stir in the sugar and salt. Pour in the milk mix and whisk together, then cover the bowl and leave to stand somewhere warm for about 1½ hours, or until you can see the fermentation starting.

Whisk the egg whites to soft peaks and fold lightly into the mix.

Now to cook the blinis. In a large, heavy-based frying pan 26cm in diameter, heat a knob of butter and a splash of oil. On a high heat, place heaped tablespoons of the mix in the frying pan, leaving a little room between them as they will spread out a bit, then turn down the heat to low and fry on each side for about 2–3 minutes, until golden brown. Place on kitchen paper to drain. You will need to cook the blinis in four or five batches. They can be kept warm on a baking tray in a low oven if serving all at once, or reheated at a later date.

Serve hot or warm, with toppings of your choice. I love the traditional smoked salmon and soured cream.

SODA BREAD

This bread uses bicarbonate of soda to rise, not yeast, and requires only a quick mix by hand and a very short resting time (5 minutes). It is a really quick bread to pull out of the bag and also has a great texture and crust and a beautiful flavour.

Preheat the oven to 200°C/fan 180°C/gas 6 and line a baking tray with baking paper.

Mix all the dry ingredients in a large bowl, then add the water and buttermilk and mix together until a wet dough is formed.

Sprinkle over a little flour to help bring the dough together, then roll it into a ball and place on the prepared baking tray. Rub the oil all over the top surface of the loaf and sprinkle with oatmeal. Cut a cross through the dough about a quarter of the way through and leave to rest for 5 minutes, then bake for 35 minutes.

Take out of the oven and put on a rack to cool.

Serve with good mature Cheddar and some bread and butter pickles (see page 262), or just with butter for breakfast.

Makes one 800g loaf
Suitable for freezing (cooked loaf)
Preparation time: 10 minutes
Proving/resting time: 5 minutes
Cooking time: 35 minutes

250g coarse or standard strong
    wholemeal flour
250g self-raising flour, plus extra
    for dusting
80g coarse or medium oatmeal,
    plus a little extra for sprinkling
6g bicarbonate of soda
12g fine sea salt
12g soft light brown sugar
200g water
250ml buttermilk
1 teaspoon olive, rapeseed or
    vegetable oil

PUMPKIN SEED BREAD

This lovely loaf has great texture and colour. It's fantastic with a bowl of soup and great for toast.

To make the ferment, put the flour into a bowl. Mix the yeast into the water and whisk to dissolve. Add this to the flour and mix until it's a thick paste. Cover with clingfilm and pierce the clingfilm as well, then leave for 24 hours.

Preheat the oven to 180°C/fan 160°C/gas 4.

Put the pumpkin seeds on a small baking tray and toast for about 18–20 minutes, shaking the tray occasionally, until they are golden brown. Leave to cool completely, preferably for a few hours. Turn off the oven.

Put the flour and salt into a bowl and add the ferment. Put the yeast, oil and water into a bowl and whisk to dissolve the yeast. Add this to the flour.

Transfer the dough into the bowl of an electric mixer with a beater attachment (this will help to break down the seeds and release the oils – do not use a dough hook). Mix for 4 minutes on medium speed, then add the toasted pumpkin seeds and mix for a further 5 minutes, until smooth and elastic. It will be quite soft at this point.

Leave the dough in the bowl, cover with clingfilm, and leave somewhere warm for about 2 hours, or until doubled in size.

Take the dough out of the bowl, place on a floured surface and shape it into a ball. Place it in a floured proving basket and leave for another hour, or until doubled in size.

Preheat the oven to 200°C/fan 180°C/gas 6 and sprinkle a baking tray with semolina.

Gently turn out the dough on to the prepared baking tray, and sprinkle some semolina on to the loaf as well (you need to keep as much air in the dough as possible, so again be gentle). Bake for 30 minutes, or until golden brown.

Place on a rack to cool.

Makes one 800g round loaf
Suitable for freezing (raw dough or cooked loaf)
Preparation time: 15 minutes
Proving/resting time: 3 hours
Cooking time: 30 minutes

FOR THE FERMENT

110g strong white bread flour
1g fresh yeast, crumbled
110g water

FOR THE DOUGH

150g shelled green pumpkin seeds
240g strong white bread flour, plus extra for dusting
8g fine sea salt
1 batch of ferment (see above)
2g fresh yeast
4 tablespoons toasted pumpkin seed oil, including the crushed seeds (see page 251)
160g water
2–3 tablespoons semolina

THE BUNS

I originally developed these as a canapé bun for serving with various types of fillings. They are fit for royalty: I made them for Prince William and Kate's royal wedding in 2011 – for their bacon buns in the morning, then 1,000 bread rolls for lunch.

Enriched with butter, these soft buns are really good whatever size you make them – whether as a mini canapé or a lunchtime bun, a classic burger bun or a hot dog roll. They take a bit longer to cook when they're larger (15–16 minutes). They freeze very well.

Makes about 24 buns

Suitable for freezing (raw dough, raw buns or cooked buns)

Preparation time: 20 minutes

Proving/resting time: 1 hour 20 minutes

Cooking time: 10 minutes

Line a baking tray with baking paper.

Put the flour, salt and sugar into the bowl of an electric mixer and mix well. Put the yeast and water into a bowl and whisk until dissolved. Pour this into the flour, then, using the dough hook attachment, mix on a medium speed for 6–8 minutes, or until it starts coming away from the sides.

Turn off the mixer, sprinkle the dough with a little flour and let it rest in the bowl for 10 minutes – you can leave it uncovered.

Start the mixer up again on a medium speed and slowly add the butter to the dough. Once the butter is incorporated, mix on a high speed for 1 minute, then cover the bowl with clingfilm and let it rest for 10 minutes. Divide into 40g pieces, roll them into balls, and *place them on the prepared baking tray, leaving some space between them. Cover loosely with clingfilm and leave until doubled in size (about 1 hour).

Preheat the oven to 200°C/fan 180°C/gas 6.

Brush the tops of the buns with beaten egg and bake for about 10–12 minutes, or until golden brown. Check that the bases are lightly golden.

Put on a rack to cool a bit. While still warm, cut in half and fill.

600g strong white bread flour, plus extra for dusting

11g fine sea salt

44g caster sugar

22g fresh yeast, crumbled

330g water

100g softened unsalted butter, cubed

1 egg, beaten, to glaze

More ways of using the buns:

HOT DOG BUNS – depending on the size of your hot dog, shape the dough into 80–90g balls. Leave to rest for 10 minutes, then roll them into sausage shapes and follow the recipe from *.

BURGER BUNS (use mustard seeds rather than sesame seeds) – again depending on the size of your burger, shape the dough into 100g balls and follow the recipe from *. After brushing with beaten egg, sprinkle with your seeds. They will need about 15–16 minutes in the oven.

CROWTHERS' DINNER ROLLS

I worked for Philip and Shirley Crowther for many years, at a restaurant in East Sheen called Crowthers. I started when I was fifteen, washing dishes, and began cooking there a few years later. My first job was to bake these lovely dinner rolls every day.

Put the flours, cubed lard or butter, salt, seeds, spring onions and parsley into the bowl of an electric mixer and mix well to combine. Put 425g of the water into a jug or bowl, add the yeast and black treacle, and whisk until the yeast has dissolved.

Pour the liquid into the flour, then, using the dough hook attachment, mix on medium speed for 6–8 minutes, or until the dough starts coming away from the sides. Add the remaining 100g of water as needed, if the dough looks dry (you may not need any).

Turn off the mixer, cover the bowl with clingfilm and leave in a warm place until doubled in size (about 2 hours).

Line a couple of baking trays with baking paper. Divide the dough into 60–65g pieces (you should get between 23 and 25 of them), roll them into balls and place on the prepared baking trays, leaving some space between them. Cover with a clean tea-towel or loosely with clingfilm. Leave until doubled in size (about 1–1½ hours).

Preheat the oven to 200°C/fan 180°C/gas 6.

Brush the tops of the rolls with beaten egg and bake for about 10–12 minutes, or until golden brown.

Remove from the tray and place on a rack to cool.

Makes about 25
Suitable for freezing (raw dough or cooked rolls)
Preparation time: 25 minutes
Proving/resting time: 3 hours
Cooking time: 12 minutes

500g strong granary bread flour
400g strong white bread flour
40g lard or butter, or half and half, cubed
20g fine sea salt
1 tablespoon sesame seeds
1 tablespoon black poppy seeds
2 tablespoons finely sliced spring onions
2 tablespoons chopped fresh curly parsley
425–525g water
15g fresh yeast, crumbled
3 tablespoons black treacle
1 egg, beaten, to glaze

CLASSIC BRIOCHE

This soft bread is enriched with butter – lots of butter (actually a whole pack, but it's well worth it). One of the best smells in a bakery is when the brioche comes out of the oven and floods the air with its sweet buttery aroma. It's great to use for eggy bread, but most famous toasted and served with a pâté or terrine.

Makes one 750g loaf
Suitable for freezing (cooked loaf)
Preparation time: 25 minutes
Proving/resting time: 3 hours,
    plus overnight
Cooking time: 25 minutes

500g strong white bread flour
12g fine sea salt
30g caster sugar
15g fresh yeast, crumbled
6 eggs
250g softened unsalted butter,
    plus extra for greasing
1 egg, beaten, to glaze

Put the flour, salt and sugar into the bowl of an electric mixer. Crumble the yeast into a bowl and break in the eggs. Whisk the eggs and yeast together to dissolve the yeast. Pour the egg mixture into the dry ingredients, then, using a dough hook attachment, mix on a medium speed for 6–8 minutes, or until the dough starts coming away from the sides. Turn off the mixer and let the dough rest for 5 minutes.

Start the mixer up again on a medium speed and while it is running slowly add the butter to the dough, a little at a time, until it is incorporated (don't add the butter too quickly, otherwise it will ruin the dough). Once the butter is incorporated, mix on high speed for 4 minutes, until the dough is glossy, smooth and elastic when pulled, then cover the bowl with clingfilm and leave until it has doubled in size (this will take about 2 hours). Knock back the dough, then re-cover and put into the fridge overnight to chill.

The next day, grease a 750g loaf tin, measuring about 28cm x 12cm x 10cm. Take the dough out of the fridge, mould it into a loaf shape and place it in the prepared tin, pressing the dough down into each corner so that it is even. Leave somewhere warm to prove until it reaches the top of the tin, which will take about 3 hours.

Preheat the oven to 180°C/fan 160°C/gas 4.

Glaze the brioche with the beaten egg and bake for 20 minutes, then take it out of the tin and put it directly on the oven shelf for another 5 minutes.

Put on a rack to cool a little, and serve warm or toasted, with a good quality pâté and some pickled beetroot (see page 261).

MADELEINES

I started baking these madeleines over ten years ago. They are still on the menu at both St John Restaurant and St John Bread & Wine, and every order is freshly baked and served straight from the oven. You really need a madeleine tray for this recipe, though you could bake them in a muffin tray if you absolutely must. Remember to serve them straight from the oven, steaming hot.

Put the honey and butter into a small saucepan and melt them together on a low heat, stirring. Take off the heat and allow to cool a little.

Place the eggs and both sugars in the bowl of an electric mixer with a whisk attachment and whiz on a high speed for about 5 minutes, until tripled in volume. Fold in the melted butter and honey. Once incorporated, add the sifted flour and baking powder and fold in again until all is incorporated. Put into the fridge to rest for at least 4 hours or overnight.

Preheat the oven to 200°C/fan 180°C/gas 6 and grease and flour a madeleine tray, tapping out any excess flour.

Spoon 1 tablespoon of the mix into each mould so that it is almost level with the rim, and bake for 10–11 minutes. Take out and serve straight away while still hot – great as an instant pudding. You can serve them with hot chocolate sauce for dipping.

You could also stir some hazelnut praline (see page 247) or rum-soaked raisins (see page 240) into the mix just before you bake them.

Makes about 24
Suitable for freezing (cooked cakes)
Preparation time: 20 minutes
Proving/resting time: 4 hours,
    or overnight
Cooking time: 11 minutes

45g clear honey
160g unsalted butter
4 eggs
150g caster sugar
20g demerara sugar
160g plain flour, sifted
10g baking powder
softened butter and plain flour,
    for the tray

PRUNE AND WALNUT LOAF

Sweet or savoury, this is great to serve with any cheese, or on its own as a cake (with a glass of whisky), or warm with custard as a pudding. It keeps really well for up to five days.

Put the prunes into a large bowl. Put the water, black treacle and butter into a medium saucepan on a medium heat and bring to a light simmer. Take off the heat, add the bicarbonate of soda (it will fizz up a little), and pour over the prunes. Cover with clingfilm and leave for 2 hours.

Preheat the oven to 180°C/fan 160°C/gas 4. Line the base and sides of a 900g loaf tin (22cm x 11cm x 7cm) with baking paper.

Stir the brown sugar, beaten eggs and walnuts into the prunes, then mix in the sifted self-raising flour until all is incorporated.

Put the mixture into the prepared loaf tin and bake for 25–30 minutes, until it is firm to the touch and a skewer comes out clean.

Serves 8–10

Not suitable for freezing

Preparation time: 15 minutes

Proving/resting time: 2 hours

Cooking time: 30 minutes

225g pitted dried ready-to-eat prunes, left whole

150g water

100g black treacle

50g butter, cubed

1 teaspoon bicarbonate of soda

50g dark brown sugar

2 eggs, beaten

175g walnut pieces

225g self-raising flour, sifted

LARDY CAKE

It's not cake, it's bread, but I like it. Lardy cake has a fabulous texture which is both light inside and crispy on the outside, with perfect spicing and sweetness.

Line a baking tray with baking paper.

Put the currants, sugars, spices and lemon zest into a bowl and mix well.

After the white dough has had its 30-minute prove, roll it out on a lightly floured surface into a rectangle 1cm thick, 40cm long and 20cm wide. Place small knobs of lard all over the rolled-out dough, then sprinkle over the currant and spice mix and press it into the dough evenly, over the lard. Fold the rectangle into thirds, by folding each end to the middle, and flip it over. Place on the prepared baking tray and cover loosely.

Rest the dough for 1 hour, then repeat the folding. Rest for another 1 hour and repeat the folding again, then let the dough rest for 30 minutes, covered loosely.

Grease two loaf tins measuring 20cm x 12cm x 8cm. Cut the dough in half and place with the cut side facing upwards in your prepared tins. Loosely cover with clingfilm, then leave to prove until the dough just reaches the tops of the tins (about 2 hours).

Preheat the oven to 180°C/fan 160°C/gas 4.

Remove the clingfilm and bake for 30 minutes.

Remove from the tins straight away but be very careful, as there is a lot of melted fat in the tins – by removing the breads straight away you can maintain the crispness on the outside and prevent sogginess.

Serve warm.

Makes 2 loaves (8 slices in each)
Not suitable for freezing
Preparation time: 40 minutes
Proving/resting time: 5 hours
Cooking time: 30 minutes

120g currants
60g caster sugar
60g demerara sugar
1 teaspoon ground mixed spice
½ teaspoon ground cinnamon
a pinch of ground ginger
zest of 1 lemon
1 batch of the baker's white tin loaf dough (see page 50)
plain flour, for dusting
200g lard, cut into small dice

CORN BREAD

Great to serve at barbecues or for picnics. If you have any leftovers, fry them with bacon for breakfast.

Preheat the oven to 200°C/fan 180°C/gas 6. Lightly oil a 20cm square cake tin 4 cm deep, preferably one with a loose base.

Put the cornmeal, flour, salt, pepper and baking powder into a large bowl.

Put the butter and milk into a small pan and warm until the butter has melted, then straight away pour over the dry mix, whisking together. Whisk in the beaten eggs.

Add the spring onions and sweetcorn and stir them into the mix. Pour the corn bread mix into the prepared cake tin, evening out the surface with the back of a spoon, and bake for 30 minutes, until golden brown.

Take out of the oven and leave to stand for 10 minutes, then remove from the tin and place on a rack to cool.

Great served warm, with barbecued ribs.

Makes one 900g square loaf
Suitable for freezing
    (cooked loaf)
Preparation time: 15 minutes
Cooking time: 30 minutes

225g cornmeal
100g self-raising flour
1 teaspoon fine sea salt
½ teaspoon ground
    white pepper
1 teaspoon baking powder
50g butter
300ml full fat milk
2 eggs, beaten
3 spring onions, finely sliced
150g cooked fresh sweetcorn
    kernels, or drained tinned
    sweetcorn

THE BAKER'S WHITE TIN LOAF

A great loaf for the whole family – good and crusty, large enough for sandwiches, with plenty left for toast.

To make the old dough, put the flour, yeast and water into a bowl and mix to a stiff dough (about 3 minutes). Cover with clingfilm and leave to prove for 6 hours, then place in the fridge, where it will be happy for a few days.

Grease a 1.2kg loaf tin measuring about 28cm x 10cm x 12cm.

Put the flour, salt and old dough into the bowl of an electric mixer. Put the water into a small bowl or jug and whisk in the fresh yeast until dissolved, then add to the mixer bowl. Using a dough hook, mix on medium speed for 3 minutes, until a ball is formed and the dough looks smooth and elastic. Once smooth and elastic, scrape the dough on to a lightly floured surface.

Start kneading the dough – you will need to do this for about 10 minutes to develop the gluten – then roll it into a tight ball and put it back into the bowl. Cover and leave in a cool place to prove for about 30 minutes.

Divide the dough into four equal pieces and shape them into tight, firm, buttock-like balls. Place them in the prepared loaf tin and leave in a warm place to prove for 2 hours, until the dough reaches the top of the tin.

Preheat the oven to 200°C/fan 180°C/gas 6.

Bake the loaf for 25 minutes, until golden, then turn down the heat to 180°C/fan 160°C/gas 5. Take the loaf out of the tin and put it back on the oven shelf for a further 5–10 minutes.

Put on a rack to cool.

You can make a brown loaf by using strong wholemeal flour instead of white – the rest of the ingredients stay the same.

Makes one 1.2kg loaf

Suitable for freezing (raw dough or cooked loaf)

Preparation time: 15 minutes

Proving/resting time:
  2½ hours

Cooking time: 30 minutes

FOR THE OLD DOUGH

320g strong white bread flour

2g yeast

230g water

FOR THE DOUGH

540g strong white bread flour, plus extra for dusting

16g fine sea salt

490g old dough (see above)

290g water

30g yeast, crumbled

SOURDOUGH STARTER – AKA MOTHER

I started my sourdough starter fourteen years ago with rhubarb from my garden. I still have it today, and many of my friends and family keep little jars of it for me just in case something happens to it, like someone throwing it away (you know who you are!). I have divided it many times to give to friends and chefs to bake with, so my mother's family is still growing.

Don't be scared to try this – I know it's more work than just popping some yeast in, but the results are well worth it, and you can divide your starter and get your friends baking as well.

Makes 500g of starter

30g rhubarb, finely sliced
strong white bread flour
wholegrain rye flour
strong wholemeal bread flour

DAY 1
Place the rhubarb in a bowl (the rhubarb acts as a catalyst to start the fermentation). Pour on 100g of water, then mix in 50g of strong white bread flour and 50g of wholegrain rye flour to make a thick paste. Leave somewhere warm for 24 hours, loosely covered with clingfilm.

DAY 2
At around the same time the following day, mix in 50g of water, 25g of strong white bread flour and 25g of wholegrain rye flour, and leave somewhere warm, again loosely covered. If there is a skin on top, just mix it in.

DAY 3
Same as day 2.

DAY 4
You should start seeing the beginning of the active fermentation. Same as day 3.

»

DAY 5

The mother should be bubbling away and smell tangy. Stir, then pour 30g of the mother into a larger bowl and pick out any bits of rhubarb. Discard these, as the rhubarb has done its job, though it should have all broken down by now. Whisk in 125g of water, then stir in 80g of strong white bread flour, 30g of wholegrain rye flour, and 30g of strong wholemeal flour until well incorporated. Cover loosely and leave in a warm place. Discard the leftover starter – there is a fair bit but it's the price to pay to get it up and running.

DAY 6

Same as for day 5 (apart from picking out the rhubarb).

DAY 7
MAKE BREAD!

Once you have made your sourdough you can re-feed the mother and bake more, or store it in the fridge without feeding, but it will take a few days to re-start it by feeding it again as for day 5.

The mother will keep happy for many months before it needs feeding again.

SOURDOUGH

Ideally you will have a proving basket, but a bowl will be fine if you don't. You can get baskets and other baking things from www.bakerybits.com.

The sourdough is a great loaf to make because of its depth of flavour (which comes from its long fermentation). It also has a wonderful leathery and chewy crust and keeps really well. The texture is strong and robust, making it the type of bread that you can use as a utensil – brilliant for serving with terrines, anchovies, rillettes and soups. It also makes great toasted sandwiches. The king of all breads.

Makes a 1kg loaf
Suitable for freezing (cooked loaf)
Preparation time: 20 minutes
Proving/resting time: 8 hours,
   plus overnight
Cooking time: 40 minutes

400g strong white bread flour,
   plus extra for dusting
50g wholegrain rye flour
50g strong wholemeal bread flour
220g sourdough starter
   (see page 53)
350g water
14g fine sea salt
a little semolina

Put the flours, sourdough starter and water into the bowl of an electric mixer with a dough hook attachment and mix together on low speed for 2 minutes. Turn it up to medium speed and mix for 4 minutes, until a ball is formed – it will be a bit sticky. Leave to rest for 20 minutes in the bowl, uncovered, then add the salt, turn on the mixer to medium speed again and mix for a further 6 minutes.

Take the dough out of the bowl and place it on a lightly floured surface. Shape into a ball, then pat it out to flatten it. Fold it into thirds, bottom to middle, then top over to bottom, and flip it over so that the seam is on the bottom. Dust with flour and cover. This starts the sourdough bulk fermentation. Every 30 minutes for the next 2 hours, do another fold, so you will have made 5 folds altogether.

After the final fold leave the dough for 1 hour, then roll it into a tight ball and leave for another 1 hour (this is the pre-shape). After that hour, again reshape it into a tight ball, place it top down in the floured proving basket/bowl and leave to prove for 6–8 hours. Alternatively, after the pre-shape you can place the dough in the fridge for an overnight fermentation of about 10 hours (this will add a more tangy flavour to your bread).

In the morning, put the dough on a lightly floured surface and form it into a tight ball. Place it top down in the floured proving basket/bowl and leave to prove for 8–10 hours.

Preheat the oven to 220°C/fan 200°C/gas 7 and sprinkle a baking tray with a little semolina.

»

Sprinkle semolina on the top of the sourdough, then gently turn it out on to the prepared baking tray. Using a razor blade or very sharp knife, score a square or ring on top of the dough and place it in the oven. Splash a few tablespoons of water in the bottom of the oven (to make some steam), then close the door quickly. Bake for 30 minutes, then take off the tray, place directly on an oven rack, and bake for a further 10 minutes. Remove from the oven when golden brown and place on a rack to cool.

NOTE: if you want to use spelt in this recipe instead of flour, you can follow the same recipe and method but it will be very sticky and hard to handle at first. By the end of the folding, however, it will be fine. Don't cut the top of the dough before it goes into the oven, as it will have a natural tear. This bread has a nice deep nutty flavour, and the spelt has a type of gluten that we are more tolerant to.

RYE AND MALT SOURDOUGH

If you are using the rye grain you will need to start this bread a day in advance, as you need to leave it to soak for 24 hours.

If using the rye grain, first preheat the oven to 180°C/fan 160°C/gas 4. Put the rye seeds on a baking tray and toast until golden brown (15–20 minutes), shaking occasionally. Pour them into a metal bowl and straight away pour the water over them. Leave for 24 hours, then drain.

Put the flour, rye flakes or soaked rye grain (reserving some for the top), sourdough starter, malt extract and water into the bowl of an electric mixer with a dough hook attachment and mix together on low speed for 2 minutes, until a ball is formed – it will be a bit sticky. Leave for 10 minutes to rest, uncovered, in the bowl, then add the salt, turn on the mixer again and mix for a further 4 minutes on medium speed. Take the dough out of the bowl and put it on a lightly floured surface. Shape it into a ball (it will be quite sticky and a little hard to handle), then place in a floured bowl, sprinkle it with more flour and cover. Leave to prove for 3 hours, then shape it into a tight ball again. Place it top down in the floured proving basket/bowl and leave to prove for 2½ hours.

Preheat the oven to 200°C/fan 180°C/gas 6.

Sprinkle some rye flour on the top of the sourdough, then gently turn it out on to a baking tray and shape it into an oval loaf roughly 25cm x 15cm. Sprinkle it with a little more rye flour and the reserved rye flakes or grain and place it in the oven. Splash a few tablespoons of water in the bottom of the oven (to make some steam), then close the door quickly. Bake for 40 minutes, then turn down the oven to 180°C/fan 160°C/gas 4. Take the loaf off the tray, place it directly on an oven rack and bake for a further 20 minutes. Remove from the oven and place on a rack to cool. Best to leave until the next day before eating, as the crumb can be a bit soft and 'gummy'.

Great with smoked fish or for making a sandwich with garlic sausage and plum ketchup (see page 255). Also makes amazing croutons.

Makes one 1kg loaf

Preparation time: 40 minutes
(excluding starter)

Proving/resting time: 5½ hours

Cooking time: 1 hour

100g rye grain + 80g water
(optional), or you can
use 100g rye flakes

500g rye flour, plus extra
for dusting

220g sourdough starter
(see page 53)

1 tablespoon liquid malt extract

300g water

15g fine sea salt

SAVOURY BAKING

I spent many years working as a chef before I started specializing in pastry and baking, and I still really enjoy savoury baking. Making things like pies and sausage rolls is a nice change from being knee-deep in sugar.

I do a lot of savoury baking at home, as it's good for lunch and supper dishes and great for experimenting with different herbs and flavours – it's always good to grow some herbs in your garden or window box, as they really help in savoury baking.

I love the creative side of savoury baking – the Otter Camp pasties came from just using what was to hand and playing around with flavours. I'd recommend that you play with the flavours in these recipes a little too: change the pizza toppings, use different cheeses in the pies and scones, and try different fillings in the buns.

With this chapter, as in Baking and Bread (page 29), I always use fresh yeast that has been crumbled up and dissolved in water – if you are using dried yeast, use half the yeast amount given in the recipe. I also always use a good fine sea salt and cold water from the tap.

I always weigh the water when making savoury bread; it's a lot more accurate than a measuring jug.

When rolling out pastry like puff, always be confident and show the pastry who is boss. Always try to roll in one direction, in one stroke.

Don't be scared to bake for a little longer to get a deep brown colour. That's what I call 'French brown' – it gives a great depth of flavour to your finished bake.

TRUFFLE, CHEESE AND POTATO PIE

This recipe takes the humble potato and turns it into a rich, luxurious and decadent pie. For a slightly less luxurious version, you can just use truffle oil (as truffles are expensive).

Put the flour and salt into the bowl of an electric mixer with a beater attachment, then add the beaten egg and warm melted butter and mix together. Slowly add the warm water and mix until you have a soft pliable dough. Cover the bowl with clingfilm and leave in a warm place to rest for 25 minutes.

Preheat the oven to 180°C/fan 160°C/gas 4. Grease an 18cm cake tin 5cm deep, with a removable base, and line the base with baking paper.

Cut off one-third of the pastry and set aside to make the lid.

Roll out the rest of the pastry into a circle about 28–30cm across and about 2mm thick and line the prepared cake tin, leaving 1cm overhanging.

Slice the potatoes and Brie 0.5cm thick. Put a layer of sliced potatoes in the bottom of the tin and add some seasoning. Follow with a layer of sliced Brie, then some slices of truffle and a dash of truffle oil. Repeat the layers until you reach the top of the tin.

Roll out the pastry for the lid, place it on top, and trim it so it fits and covers the filling. Eggwash, then fold the overhanging pastry over the lid and seal.

Put it into the fridge to rest for 10 minutes, then place on a baking tray and bake for 30–35 minutes, until golden brown.

Serve with pickled tomatoes (see page 258).

Serves 6
Not suitable for freezing
Preparation time: 25 minutes
Cooking time: 35 minutes
  (excluding the potatoes)

FOR THE PASTRY

250g strong white bread flour,
  plus extra for dusting
a pinch of fine sea salt
1 egg, beaten
50g warm melted unsalted butter
100ml warm water
1 egg, beaten, to glaze

FOR THE FILLING

4 large potatoes, cooked in their
  skins, peeled
200g Brie (or you can use
  a truffle Brie, but in that case
  leave out the black truffles)
fine sea salt and black pepper
2 or 3 small black truffles
4 teaspoons truffle oil

PUFF PASTRY

This recipe makes a big batch of puff pastry – it takes a while, so you may as well make a big batch and freeze it so that you have some up your sleeve. I know you can buy good puff pastry from the shops and that making it yourself is a long process, but homemade really does make a massive difference. You can use the puff pastry for many things: anchovy twists and cheese straws (see page 69), sausage rolls (see page 66), or as a topping for pies and vol-au-vent bases.

Makes about 2kg
Suitable for freezing
Preparation time: 1 hour,
    plus chilling time

1kg strong white bread flour,
    plus extra for dusting
15g fine sea salt
250g cold unsalted butter, diced
375–450ml cold water
25ml white wine vinegar
750g softened unsalted butter

Place the flour, salt and diced cold butter in the bowl of an electric mixer with a beater attachment and mix on low speed until the mixture looks like fine breadcrumbs.

Change the attachment to a dough hook and gradually add the cold water (beginning with the lesser amount and adding more as it's needed) and vinegar, then mix on a medium speed for about 2 minutes. It should feel nice and pliable.

Take the dough out of the bowl, wrap it in clingfilm and put it into the fridge to rest for at least 2 hours or overnight.

Take the butter out of the fridge to soften, and when it's been out for 15 minutes or so, take out the dough: the dough and butter need to be the same softness (this is very important).

Roll out the dough on a lightly floured surface into the shape of a cross measuring about 45cm, leaving the centre thicker than the flaps which make the arms of the cross, then dot the butter evenly over the centre of the dough and fold over the flaps to enclose it. Fold over the top and bottom flaps first, then cover with the side flaps to make sure no butter is showing – and if the flaps are not long enough to cover the butter, just roll them out a little longer.

Start rolling lengthways until you have a strip 60cm long and 20cm wide, brushing off any excess flour and making sure all the sides are straight.

With one of the shorter sides towards you, fold it into thirds, first bottom to middle, then top over to bottom – this finishes the first turn. Turn the pastry so that the seam or join is always on the right, and roll out again just as before – this is the second turn.

Wrap the pastry in clingfilm and put it into the fridge for 3 hours. Then repeat another two turns as above, again resting for 3 hours. Finally put two more turns in, so in total you have done six turns. Rest the pastry again before you use it.

SAUSAGE ROLLS

This recipe makes four different sausage rolls: classic, garlic, chilli and black pudding. You can cut them to whatever size you like, small, medium or large.

Preheat the oven to 180°C/fan 160°C/gas 4 and line a baking tray with baking paper.

Put the filling ingredients into four separate bowls. Season with salt and pepper and mix so you have all the fillings ready.

On a lightly floured work surface, roll out the puff pastry into a rectangle 65cm x 18cm.

Roll out each filling to a sausage shape about 14cm long and place the first one 5cm from one of the shorter ends of the rolled-out puff pastry, parallel to the edge. Then place the rest of the sausage shapes parallel to that, 3cm apart. Brush all the edges of the puff pastry and in between the fillings with egg yolk, then fold the other short end of the pastry over the sausagemeat to enclose it. Press the pastry down round the edges, then use the back of a fork dipped in flour to press down along the seam and seal the join. Finally, with your finger, press down the pastry between the rows of sausagemeat.

Cut through the pastry at right angles to make 4 sausage rolls from each row of filling, or cut the rolls to whatever size you like, then place them on the prepared baking tray and pop it into the fridge for a couple of hours to let the pastry rest.

Brush the tops of the rolls with beaten egg yolk and score the top three or four times at an angle. Bake for 30–40 minutes, until golden brown and hot throughout.

Makes 16 (4 of each kind)
Suitable for freezing
   (uncooked or cooked)
Preparation time: 20 minutes
   (excluding the pastry)
Cooking time: 30–40 minutes

600g puff pastry (to make
   your own, see page 65)
flour, for dusting
2 egg yolks, beaten, to glaze

CLASSIC
100g sausagemeat
1 tablespoon finely chopped
   fresh curly parsley
1 tablespoon finely chopped onion
½ teaspoon finely chopped fresh sage

GARLIC
100g sausagemeat
5 cloves of garlic, crushed
½ teaspoon finely chopped
   fresh thyme leaves

CHILLI
100g sausagemeat
½ a red chilli, finely chopped
2 teaspoons chilli-infused olive oil
1 tablespoon finely chopped onion

BLACK PUDDING
100g black pudding, broken up
1 tablespoon peeled and finely
   chopped apple
½ teaspoon finely chopped fresh
   tarragon leaves
a small pinch of ground mace

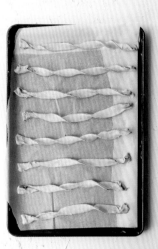

ANCHOVY TWISTS AND CHEESE STRAWS

These are great as canapés with some bubbles – you can bake them in the morning and serve them for lunch or with evening drinks. They look sublime served in tall glasses, and they are also very delicious and addictive.

I have made thousands of twists and straws for many individual wedding parties, and the glasses are always empty by the time everyone sits down for lunch or dinner.

Preheat the oven to 180°C/fan 160°C/gas 4 and line two baking trays with baking paper.

Put the anchovies into a food processor with the oil they come in and the crushed garlic, and whiz until smooth. Alternatively use a pestle and mortar.

Cut the puff pastry in half, then roll each half into a rectangle about 50cm long and 20cm wide.

To make the anchovy twists, spread the anchovy and garlic paste over half the pastry, then fold over the other side like a sandwich and chill in the fridge until firm. Once firm, eggwash the pastry, trim the edges to neaten, then cut into 1cm slices and twist them.

To make the cheese straws, spread the mustard over the second half of the pastry and sprinkle with grated cheese (pressing it down so that it sticks to the pastry). Sprinkle with cayenne pepper, then fold, chill, eggwash, cut and twist as above.

Place all the straws on the prepared baking trays and bake for 15–18 minutes, until golden brown.

Makes 40
Suitable for freezing
   (raw or frozen)
Preparation time: 20 minutes
   (excluding pastry-making time)
Cooking time: 15–18 minutes

50g anchovies in oil
1 clove of garlic, crushed
500g puff pastry (see page 65)
1 egg, beaten, to glaze
1 tablespoon Dijon mustard
110g mature Cheddar cheese,
   finely grated
½ teaspoon cayenne pepper

CHEESE AND SMOKED PAPRIKA SCONES

I normally serve these scones either as a snack (just with butter) or as a teatime sandwich, with cheese and piccalilli. You can try different cheeses if you like.

Makes about 12–14
Suitable for freezing (cooked)
Preparation time: 15 minutes
Cooking time: 10–12 minutes

Preheat the oven to 200°C/fan 180°C/gas 6 and line a baking tray with baking paper.

Put the flour, bicarbonate of soda, cream of tartar, caster sugar, both paprikas, mustard powder, butter and salt into a large bowl and rub together with your fingertips until the butter is incorporated into the flour.

Stir in the Cheddar, then add the buttermilk and mix together until the dough begins to take shape – bring it together with your hands but do not over-mix. Then let it rest for 5 minutes.

On a lightly floured work surface, roll out the dough to a thickness of 2cm and cut out scones using a 6cm fluted pastry cutter. Place them on the prepared baking tray and glaze with the beaten egg, then sprinkle with the Parmesan and bake for 10–12 minutes, until golden brown. Put on a rack to cool.

Serve warm, with plenty of butter or cheese and piccalilli (see page 254). Eat them on the day they're made.

500g plain flour, plus extra
  for dusting
2 teaspoons bicarbonate of soda
2 teaspoons cream of tartar
2 teaspoons caster sugar
2 teaspoons sweet smoked
  paprika
1 teaspoon picante (hot) paprika
1 teaspoon English mustard
  powder
80g cold unsalted butter, diced
2 teaspoons fine sea salt
200g strong Cheddar cheese,
  finely grated
320ml buttermilk
1 egg, beaten, to glaze
2 tablespoons finely grated
  Parmesan cheese

SWEET ONION AND FINE HERB TART

This is great for summer picnics, as its crisp buttery pastry holds together well so that it can be picked up by hand and eaten easily. Also great as a starter, served warm.

Put the flour, salt and butter into a food processor and whiz until it looks like breadcrumbs. Add the milk and whiz until it forms a dough. Wrap in clingfilm and put into the fridge to rest for a couple of hours.

Preheat the oven to 180°C/fan 160°C/gas 4. Grease a 23cm tart case 3cm deep and line it with baking paper.

Take the pastry out of the fridge to soften for about 20 minutes, then roll it out to a circle 3mm thick and large enough to fit the prepared tart case. Line the tart case with the pastry and chill in the freezer for 1 hour, then put it on a baking tray and bake blind (line the pastry with baking paper and fill the base with baking beans) for 12 minutes. Remove the paper and baking beans and bake for about another 12 minutes until golden brown. Leave to cool completely. Reduce the oven temperature to 160°C/fan 140°C/gas 3.

Meanwhile, heat the butter and olive oil in a heavy-based saucepan and add the onions and bay leaves. Cook gently with a lid on, on a medium-low heat, for about 20 minutes, stirring occasionally. Then take off the lid, turn up the heat and cook for a further 10 minutes, or until the juice from the onions has nearly gone, watching out that it doesn't catch on the bottom of the saucepan (you do not want any colour on the onions). Remove the bay leaves and leave the onions to cool completely.

Once the onions have cooled, put them into a large bowl. Add the herbs, spring onions, egg, egg yolk and cream and whisk together. Season with salt and pepper. Pour into the tart case and bake for 15 minutes, then turn up the heat to 200°C/fan 180°C/gas 6 and bake for a further 5 minutes.

Remove the tart from the oven and leave to stand for 10 minutes or until completely cool, but do not refrigerate.

Serve cold or warm, with tomato and chilli chutney (see page 253) and pickled onions (see page 256).

Feeds about 8, or 4 if everyone's
  hungry and has seconds
Not suitable for freezing
Preparation time: 30 minutes,
  plus chilling time
Cooking time: 45 minutes

FOR THE SHORTCRUST PASTRY
250g plain flour
a pinch of fine sea salt
150g cold unsalted butter,
  diced small
50ml full fat milk

FOR THE FILLING
40g butter
2 tablespoons olive oil
6 large onions, finely sliced
2 bay leaves
3 tablespoons chopped fresh parsley
1 tablespoon chopped fresh dill
1 tablespoon chopped fresh chives
1 teaspoon chopped fresh tarragon
2 spring onions, finely chopped
1 egg
1 egg yolk
100ml double cream
1 teaspoon fine sea salt
¼ teaspoon white pepper

OTTER CAMP PASTIES

This recipe came from a fishing trip near Lechlade, where we caught lots of crayfish which we ate nearly every day for lunch, steamed in herbs and white wine. On our last day we pulled up the nets and found not only lots of crayfish but also a brown trout, so we took it all home and came up with these pasties.

Makes 5 pasties
Not suitable for freezing
Preparation time: 50 minutes,
    plus chilling time
Cooking time: 35 minutes

Put the flour, salt and butter into a food processor and whiz until it looks like breadcrumbs. Add the milk and whiz until you have a dough. Wrap it in clingfilm and put it into the fridge to rest for a couple of hours.

Fillet, pin-bone and trim the trout, then slice each fillet into three. (Keep the bones and trimmings for the stock.)

Put all the cooking liquid ingredients into a large saucepan, including the fish bones and trimmings, and bring to the boil. Reduce the heat and simmer for 2 minutes, then add the raw crayfish, if using. Put a lid on the pan and simmer for 5 minutes, shaking occasionally, then leave the crayfish to cool in the stock.

Once cool, peel the crayfish. Twist off the head away from the body and discard, then break open the soft shell along the belly and smash the body with the flat side of a large cook's knife. Peel the shell away from the flesh, then run the tip of a small knife down the back of the crayfish to expose the intestine tube, pull it away from the flesh and discard. Cut the tail into 3 pieces, and leave the claws whole.

To make the sauce, pour the cooking liquid through a fine sieve into a saucepan. Put it on a high heat and boil for about 5 minutes, until reduced to about 175ml. Melt the butter in a heavy-based saucepan, then stir in the flour and cook on a low heat for 2–3 minutes. Gradually whisk in the reduced stock, bring to a gentle simmer, then pass through a sieve into a large bowl. Leave to cool completely.

Slice the cooked potatoes and put them into a large bowl. Roughly chop the watercress and add to the bowl, then add the cooked and prepared crayfish (or ready-cooked crayfish, if using) and the chopped dill, wood sorrel and spring onions. Season with sea salt, freshly ground black pepper and the lemon juice, then stir in the sauce and gently fold in the 6 bits of trout. Check the seasoning again.

FOR THE SHORTCRUST PASTRY

250g plain flour
a pinch of fine sea salt
150g cold unsalted butter, diced small
50ml full fat milk
2 egg yolks, beaten, to glaze

FOR THE FILLING

1 x 400g whole prepared trout
6 large raw crayfish (alternatively, use 150g cooked shelled crayfish tails or 12 large tiger prawns)
250g Charlotte potatoes, peeled and cooked
a handful of watercress
1 tablespoon chopped fresh dill
a pinch of chopped fresh wood sorrel (or normal sorrel)
2 spring onions, finely chopped
a pinch of fine sea salt
freshly ground black pepper
juice of 1 lemon

Take the pastry out of the fridge to soften so you can roll it out.

Preheat the oven to 200°C/fan 180°C/gas 6 and line a baking tray with baking paper.

Roll out the pastry to a thickness of 3mm and cut out four 15cm circles, using a saucer as a guide. Roll out the trimmings and cut out one more, then eggwash the rims of the five circles and divide the filling equally between them, placing it on half of the circle.

Fold over the pastry to enclose the filling and press down to seal, then lift up the edges and crimp together. Place on the prepared baking tray and chill in the fridge for 10–15 minutes, then glaze with egg yolk and bake for 20 minutes, until piping hot and golden brown.

Serve with wedges of lemon and some pickled beetroot (see page 261).

FOR THE COOKING LIQUID

300ml white wine

100ml water

2 bay leaves

1 teaspoon fennel seeds

1 star anise

1 clove of garlic, smashed

1 strip of lemon peel

5 or 6 black peppercorns

a pinch of fine sea salt

3 stalks of fresh dill

the trout bones and trimmings

FOR THE SAUCE

15g unsalted butter

15g plain white flour

BACON AND CORN MUNCHIES

These are great as a canapé or starter, but are best as a snack with a few cold beers. Nice dipped into plum ketchup (see page 255).

First slice your bacon into lardons and dry-fry it in a pan until golden and crispy. Drain on kitchen paper and leave to cool.

Sift the flour and salt into a large bowl.

Whisk the egg yolk and milk together.

Slowly add the milk mix to the flour mix and whisk together until smooth, then add the crispy bacon, sweetcorn, chopped parsley and pepper and stir together.

Whisk the egg white until firm and fold into the sweetcorn mix.

Preheat oil to 180°C in a deep-fat fryer or a large saucepan. Working in batches of 3 or 4 at a time, drop in a serving spoonful of the mixture and fry for 3 minutes on each side.

Once cooked, drain on kitchen paper and sprinkle with salt and picante paprika.

Great served hot, with some ice-cold beers.

Makes 15 two-bite pieces
Not suitable for freezing
Preparation time: 15 minutes
Cooking time: 10 minutes

3 rashers of smoked
    thick-cut bacon
110g plain flour
a pinch of fine sea salt
1 egg, separated
150ml full fat milk
160g cooked or tinned and
    drained sweetcorn
a generous pinch of chopped
    curly parsley
a good couple of twists of
    black pepper
2 litres sunflower or vegetable
    oil, for frying
fine sea salt and picante (hot)
    paprika, for sprinkling

BACON AND GARLIC BREAD

This is a good sharing bread and goes really well with pasta dishes or soups. Just place it in the middle of your table and watch it disappear.

To make the ferment, put the three ingredients into a bowl and mix together. Cover with clingfilm and leave for 24 hours.

Cut the bacon into small pieces and gently fry them in a heavy-based saucepan until they are nice and crispy. Add the garlic and olive oil and continue to cook on a low heat until soft. Stir in the chopped rosemary and thyme and leave to cool in the pan (do not drain the fat off, as it will go into the dough).

Put the water into a bowl and whisk in the yeast until dissolved, then put into the bowl of an electric mixer with a dough hook attachment. Add the ferment and the flour and mix on a medium speed for 6 minutes, or until it starts coming away from the sides.

Turn off the mixer and let the dough rest for 5 minutes. Add the salt and mix for a further 4 minutes, until smooth.

Shape the dough into a ball, then place it in an oiled bowl and cover with clingfilm. Put it in a warm place for about 1 hour, until it has doubled in size.

On a lightly floured surface, shape the dough into a rectangle about 40cm x 25cm. Spoon the bacon and garlic mix over half the dough, lengthways. Fold the rest of the dough over and seal the edges, then roll it up, starting at one of the shorter sides. Place it in the pan you cooked your bacon in, cover, and leave for 1 hour, until doubled in size again.

Flatten the dough into a rectangle again, then, with one of the shorter ends facing you, fold it into thirds, first top to middle, then bottom to top. Flip it over, then put it back into the bacon pan, cover and leave for 1 hour. Meanwhile grease a baking tin measuring about 28cm x 12cm x 10cm.

After an hour, repeat as above but put the dough into the prepared baking tin. Cover and leave until the dough just reaches the top of the tin (about 2 hours).

Preheat the oven to 200°C/fan 180°C/gas 6. Bake for 40 minutes, then take the loaf out of the tin and bake directly on the oven shelf for a further 10 minutes. Put on a rack to cool.

Serves 8
Suitable for freezing
Preparation time: 30 minutes, plus proving time
Cooking time: 50 minutes

FOR THE FERMENT
50g strong white bread flour
50g water
1g fresh yeast

FOR THE DOUGH
300g smoked streaky bacon
20 cloves of garlic, peeled and thinly sliced
1 tablespoon olive oil
1 teaspoon chopped fresh rosemary
1 teaspoon chopped fresh thyme leaves
360g water
5g fresh yeast, crumbled
1 batch of ferment (see above)
500g strong white bread flour, plus extra for dusting
12g fine sea salt

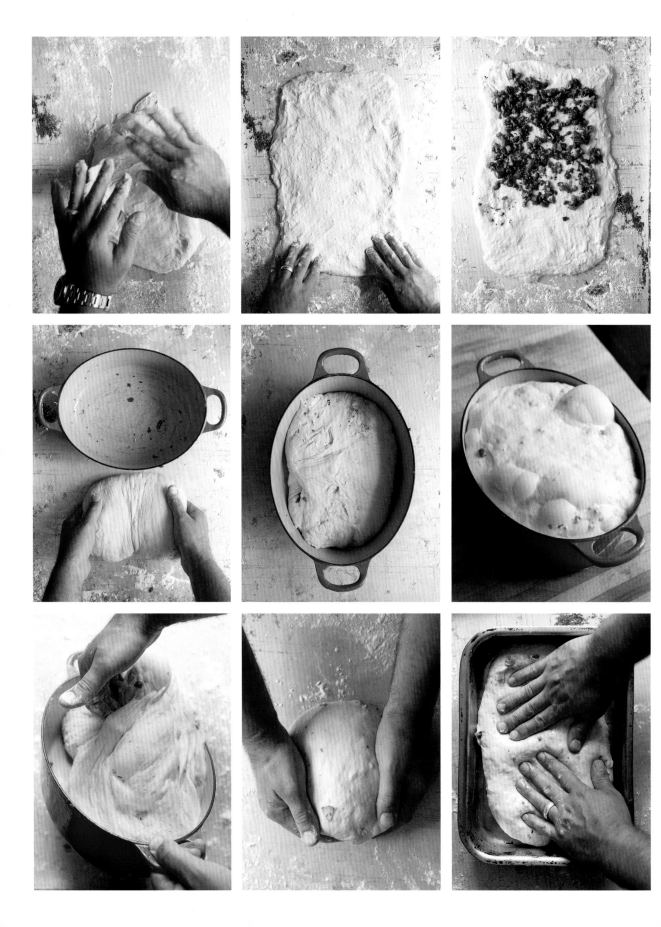

OLIVE OIL BUNS

The olive oil gives these buns a really light and airy texture. They are so moist that they will keep happily for a few days (or longer if toasted) – great for making little sandwich buns. Cut the dough into smaller pieces for canapé size buns.

To make the ferment, put the three ingredients into a bowl and mix together. Cover with clingfilm and leave for 24 hours.

Put the water into a bowl and whisk in the yeast until dissolved, then put into the bowl of an electric mixer with a dough hook attachment. Add the ferment, flour and salt, and mix on a medium speed for 6 minutes, or until the dough starts coming away from the sides. With the machine on high speed, gradually pour in all but 2 tablespoons of the oil, and keep mixing until it's smooth, glossy and elastic when pulled (it will be a very wet dough).

Place the dough in an olive-oiled bowl, cover and leave for 1 hour. When the hour is up, add the reserved 2 tablespoons of olive oil, a tablespoon at a time, mixing it in by hand. Flatten the dough into a rectangle, then, with one of the shorter ends facing you, fold it into thirds, first bottom to middle, then top to bottom. Flip it over, then cover and leave for one more hour.

When the hour is up, divide the dough into 50g pieces and put them into the holes in an olive-oiled 12-hole muffin tray. Try to mould a smooth surface on top of each bun – I know it's very wet, but flouring your hands lightly should make it easier. Then leave the buns somewhere warm for about 1 hour, or until just before they reach the top of the moulds.

Preheat the oven to 220°C/fan 200°C/gas 7 and bake for 15 minutes. Remove the buns from the oven and place on a rack to cool.

Serve them warm on their own, or use them to make little sandwich buns.

Makes 12
Suitable for freezing
Preparation time: 30 minutes, plus proving time
Cooking time: 15 minutes

FOR THE FERMENT
65g strong white bread flour
65g water
1g fresh yeast

FOR THE DOUGH
200g warm water
4g fresh yeast, crumbled
1 batch of ferment (see above)
250g strong white bread flour, plus extra for dusting
7g fine sea salt
85ml olive oil

CHEESE AND CHILLI POPS

These amazing cheese and chilli bread rolls always bring back fond memories, as I first ate them on honeymoon in America, in a restaurant in the Grand Canyon. As soon as we got home I developed these pops using a brioche dough.

Once the brioche has had its overnight prove, line two baking trays with baking paper.

Finely chop the chillies (including the seeds) and mix them into the dough. Cut the dough into 40g pieces and place them on the prepared baking trays, leaving space between them. Eggwash and grate Parmesan all over the tops of the rolls, then cover loosely and leave somewhere warm to prove.

Once doubled in size, which will take about 3 hours, preheat the oven to 200°C/fan 180°C/gas 6 and bake for 15 minutes, until golden brown. Cook in batches if necessary.

Serve warm.

Makes about 30
Suitable for freezing
Preparation time: 45 minutes,
    plus proving and chilling time
Cooking time: 15 minutes

1 batch of classic brioche dough
    (see page 43)
50g green chillies
1 egg, beaten, to glaze
70g Parmesan cheese,
    or a good strong Cheddar

GELLATLY PIZZA OR CALZONE

There are some good pizza stones available which really help to evenly distribute the heat for that authentic, really crispy base, but you can use a baking tray too. It's best to use semolina to stop the pizza sticking to the tray, as flour doesn't work. You can use whatever topping you like, but do try the Gellatly one.

Makes 1 big pizza or calzone
Not suitable for freezing
Preparation time: 25 minutes, plus proving time
Cooking time: 15 minutes

Put the water into a bowl and whisk in the yeast until dissolved, then put into the bowl of an electric mixer with a dough hook attachment. Add the flour and salt and mix for 5 minutes, until you have a smooth and elastic dough.

Scrape the dough into a bowl and rub with the olive oil. Cover the bowl loosely with clingfilm and leave to rise for 2 hours.

Once the dough has risen, divide it in half and form into two balls. Cover and leave to rest for at least 1 hour, so the dough can relax.

To make a pizza, roll out one of the pieces of dough to a circle about 30cm in diameter, and place it on a piece of baking paper dusted with semolina. Cover with a tea towel or clingfilm and leave for 35 minutes. To make a calzone, roll out the dough into a rectangle about 35cm x 25cm.

Preheat the oven to 240°C/fan 220°C/gas 9 and heat a baking tray.

If you are making a pizza, chop the tomato into small dice and gently spread them over the base, right to the edge. Slice the black pudding and lay it evenly over the tomato. Chop the chilli (include the seeds if you like it hot, or remove them if you don't want it too hot) and sprinkle it over the pizza, along with the sliced pickled garlic. Season with salt and pepper, then, using a vegetable peeler, peel strips of cheese over the whole pizza, and sprinkle with olive oil.

If you are making a calzone, do the same as above but just put the filling lengthways on half the dough. Fold the other half of the dough over the filling and seal by crimping the ends together all the way round.

Take the preheated baking tray out of the oven and sprinkle it with semolina. Slide the pizza on to the tray and bake for 8–10 minutes, until crispy. The calzone will need a little longer – about 15 minutes.

Chop the rocket and scatter it over the pizza. Sprinkle it with olive oil or, if you are feeling cheeky, a little truffle oil. With the calzone serve a little rocket salad.

325g water
6g fresh yeast, crumbled
500g strong white bread flour
10g fine sea salt
1 tablespoon olive oil, plus extra for drizzling
semolina, for sprinkling
1 ripe vine tomato
50g black pudding, sliced
1 red chilli
1–2 pickled garlic cloves (see page 259)
salt and pepper
50g Manchego cheese
a handful of rocket
truffle oil (optional)

CAKES AND TEATIME TREATS

Baking cakes is something most of us first do as children, helping out in the kitchen (even if it's just licking the bowl). From the classic Victoria sponge to a rich spicy ginger cake, everyone loves a piece of cake.

I use large eggs for all my recipes.

And I always weigh the water when making yeast buns; it's a lot more accurate than using a measuring jug.

THE KIT

You don't need to spend lots, but this is the equipment you will need:

1. Digital scales – these are a real must for precise measurements.

2. A mixer – I have a KitchenAid and a Kenwood. Both are great and really good for those light sponges, etc.

3. A 26cm round springform cake tin.

4. A 450g loaf tin.

5. Two 20cm round cake tins – perfect for those Victoria sponges.

6. A set of teaspoon measures.

7. Disposable piping bags – for filling those doughnuts and piping out butter fingers and choux buns.

8. A digital thermometer – for checking jam setting points and temperature of caramels.

9. A spatula – for light folding.

10. A wooden spoon.

11. A metal skewer – for testing that cakes are baked through.

12. A sieve – for getting those lumps out.

SOME CAKE BAKING TIPS

HOW TO CREAM BUTTER AND SUGAR
It's important that your butter is soft – if it's not, it can be difficult to combine it with the sugar. When beating your butter and sugar together, make sure you scrape down the sides of the bowl occasionally to ensure that all the sugar is incorporated. The end result should be almost white in colour.

FOLDING A MIXTURE TOGETHER
Scrape the side of the bowl with a spatula, then lift your mix and fold over gently – but don't be hesitant, as the longer you take the more air you will lose. Once all the flour has been folded in, STOP.

OPENING THE OVEN DOOR
If you can't see through your oven door glass and need to check on your cake's progress, just peek in by very slightly opening the door (not fully) and gently closing it. When the baking's nearly finished, opening the door shouldn't really matter too much.

HOW DO YOU KNOW WHEN IT'S DONE?
Gently touch your cake to see if it springs back, or insert a metal skewer into the middle. Remember to leave the skewer in for 4 seconds (don't just stick it in and out). If it comes out clean, the cake is cooked.

BE PATIENT
Remember to leave your cake to cool before trying to eat it. I know it's hard, but please wait. If you dive straight in, the texture won't be right (it will be a bit doughy) and you run the risk of the cake collapsing on itself.

SWISS ALMOND CAKE

Preheat the oven to 160°C/fan 140°C/gas 3. Lightly grease a 26cm springform cake tin and line the base and sides with baking paper.

Make the topping first: melt the butter and sugar together in a medium saucepan on a low heat, then stir in the milk, flour, ground almonds and flaked almonds, and put to one side.

Now the cake: melt the butter in a saucepan on a low heat. Whisk the eggs and sugar together, using an electric mixer, until light and fluffy, then fold in first the melted butter, then the sifted flour and baking powder, then the cream and almond extract.

Pour into the prepared cake tin and bake for 25 minutes, then remove and increase the oven temperature to 180°C/fan 160°C/gas 4. Gently and evenly spoon the topping mix over the cake and put back into the oven for 35 – 45 minutes, until it is golden brown and a skewer comes out clean.

Remove from the oven and leave to cool in the tin for 20 minutes before turning out. Either serve straight away, still warm, or leave on a rack to cool completely.

Serve with raspberries and softly whipped cream.

Serves: 8 – 10
Not suitable for freezing
Preparation time: 25 minutes
Cooking time: 1 hour 10 minutes

FOR THE CAKE

200g unsalted butter

4 eggs

300g caster sugar

400g plain flour, sifted

1 teaspoon baking powder

100ml double cream

1½ teaspoons almond extract

FOR THE TOPPING

200g butter

200g caster sugar

4 tablespoons full fat milk

4 tablespoons plain flour, sifted

50g ground almonds

200g flaked almonds

TRAVELLERS' FRUIT CAKE

My wife Louise and I named this travellers' fruit cake, as my mum brought it to us in France when we were travelling around Europe at the age of eighteen. We had it for three months and it travelled to about twenty countries, so it keeps really well. It's good for putting a smile on your face when you're waiting for your next early morning train and it's been delayed for sixteen hours (I'm still bitter).

Put the raisins, sultanas, currants, prunes, apricots and mixed peel into a large bowl. Add the orange zest and juice, brandy and rum and mix together. Cover the bowl and leave overnight, or for at least 6 hours.

Preheat the oven to 140°C/fan 120°C/gas 1. Grease a 26cm springform cake tin and double-line the base and sides.

Sift the flour and all the spices into a large bowl.

Using a mixer with a beater attachment, or in a bowl with a wooden spoon, cream your butter and sugar together until light and fluffy. Add the beaten eggs gradually, whisking all the time to prevent splitting. Beat in the black treacle, then fold in the flour and spices. Finally, mix in the soaked fruit, along with any liquid remaining in the bowl.

Pour into the prepared cake tin and smooth the top evenly. Cut a strip of newspaper about 12cm wide and long enough to go around the tin, and tie it round the outside, using string to secure it. Cut out a circle of baking paper, butter it, and place it buttered side down on the surface of the cake (if it's not buttered it sticks). Place three or four circles of newspaper on top of the baking paper.

Bake for 2 hours, then remove the newspaper and baking paper from the top and bake for a further 30 minutes – it's ready when a skewer comes out clean.

The cake is best left to completely cool in the tin. Once cool, if you're not eating it straight away, wrap it first in a couple of layers of baking paper, then tightly in foil, and store it in an airtight tin.

Keeps well for 6 months.

Makes a 26cm cake

No need to freeze

Preparation time: 40 minutes

Marinating time: 6 hours
or overnight

Cooking time: 2 hours 30 minutes

200g raisins

200g sultanas

200g currants

110g pitted prunes, chopped

175g dried apricots, chopped

75g candied cut mixed peel

zest and juice of 1 orange

100ml brandy

50ml dark rum

225g plain flour

1 teaspoon mixed spice

1 teaspoon ground cinnamon

½ teaspoon freshly grated nutmeg

¼ teaspoon ground ginger

175g soft butter, plus extra
for greasing

175g soft dark brown sugar

3 eggs, beaten

100g black treacle

VICTORIA SPONGE

The classic, and one of my favourite cakes. The addition of an extra yolk gives it a lovely richness.

Preheat the oven to 180°C/fan 160°C/gas 4. Lightly grease two 20cm sandwich tins and line the base with baking paper.

Using a mixer with a beater attachment, or in a bowl with a wooden spoon, cream your butter and sugar together until light and fluffy. Beat the eggs and yolk together in a small jug or bowl, then very slowly add them to the creamed butter and sugar, whisking all the time to prevent splitting. Fold in the sifted flour and vanilla extract until all is incorporated.

Divide the cake mix equally between the prepared tins. Smooth the mixture out to the sides of the tins and level the tops with the back of a spoon. Bake for 18–20 minutes, or until golden brown and firm to the touch.

Take out of the oven and cool in the tins for 5 minutes, then turn out on to a rack and leave to cool completely.

Once cold, spread one of the cakes with lashings of raspberry jam. Place the other one on top and dust with icing sugar.

Serves: 8
Suitable for freezing
  (without the jam)
Preparation time: 15 minutes
Cooking time: 20 minutes

180g unsalted butter, softened
180g caster sugar
3 eggs
1 egg yolk
180g self-raising flour, sifted
1 teaspoon vanilla extract

TO SERVE
3–4 tablespoons raspberry jam
  (see page 241)
1 tablespoon icing sugar

APPLE AND CALVADOS CAKE WITH MIST

I first served this cake many years ago: we used to spray the Calvados and cider on to the cake as we served it, and this became known as the 'mist'. Serve the mist in a jug and let people pour it over the cake before they eat it so that it soaks in a little and brings all the apple flavours together.

Serves 12–14
Not suitable for freezing
Preparation time: 20 minutes
Marinating time: 1 hour
Cooking time: 1¼ hours

Peel and core your apples and cut them into 1cm cubes. Put them into a bowl with the walnuts, then add the Calvados and leave for 1 hour.

Preheat the oven to 160°C/fan 140°C/gas 3. Butter a deep 26cm springform cake tin and line the base and sides with baking paper.

Put the sugar and eggs into the bowl of an electric mixer with a whisk attachment and whisk until pale and fluffy. Gradually pour in the sunflower oil (as you would when making mayonnaise), whisking continuously for about 3–4 minutes, then add the sifted flour, bicarbonate of soda, cinnamon, salt and cloves and mix well. Fold in the apples (including the juices).

Spread the cake mix evenly in the prepared tin and bake for 1¼ hours, until golden brown and firm to the touch. The cake is ready when a skewer inserted into the centre comes out clean.

Leave to cool in the tin for at least 20 minutes before turning out.

While the cake is cooling, make the mist. Pour the cider into a saucepan and warm through slightly on a low heat. Take off the heat and add the Calvados.

Serve the cake at room temperature, with cream and the warm mist.

3 large cooking apples
140g walnuts, chopped
6 tablespoons Calvados
   (apple brandy)
a knob of butter
450g caster sugar
3 eggs
350ml sunflower oil
440g plain flour, sifted
1 teaspoon bicarbonate of soda
2 teaspoons ground cinnamon
a pinch of fine sea salt
¼ teaspoon ground cloves

FOR THE MIST
250ml cider
25ml Calvados

GARDEN CAKE

This is my take on the classic carrot cake, developed in order to use up some of the courgettes and carrots from my garden. If you prefer you can use just carrots, or just courgettes, but I think a mixture works best.

Preheat the oven to 160°C/fan 140°C/gas 3. Lightly grease a 26cm springform cake tin and line the base and sides with baking paper.

Coarsely grate the carrots and courgettes into a large mixing bowl, using the large holes of a box grater. Add the walnuts and orange zest and mix well.

Using an electric mixer, beat the eggs and sugars together in a large bowl for 2 minutes. Whisk in the oil gradually, then stir in the grated carrot mix. Sift the flour, bicarbonate of soda, baking powder, nutmeg, cinnamon, ginger, cloves and salt into another large bowl and mix together well, then fold the dry ingredients into the wet mixture until all is incorporated.

Pour into the prepared cake tin and bake for about 1 hour 30 minutes, until risen, golden brown and firm to the touch.

Remove the cake from the oven and leave to cool in the tin for 20 minutes, then turn out and place on a rack to cool completely.

Once cold you can frost the cake and decorate it. Remove the cream cheese from the fridge 30 minutes before using, so that it softens. To make the frosting, beat the softened butter and sugar together for about 3 minutes, until light and fluffy, then beat in the cream cheese until smooth.

Spread the frosting over the cooled cake and scatter with your chosen leaves and flowers.

Serves: 12
Not suitable for freezing
Preparation time: 25 minutes
Cooking time: 1 hour 30 minutes

FOR THE CAKE
125g carrots
125g courgettes
140g walnuts, chopped
zest of 1 orange
4 eggs
220g caster sugar
220g soft light brown sugar
300ml rapeseed oil
300g plain flour
½ teaspoon bicarbonate of soda
½ teaspoon baking powder
½ teaspoon grated nutmeg
½ teaspoon ground cinnamon
½ teaspoon ground ginger
a pinch of ground cloves
a pinch of fine sea salt

FOR THE FROSTING
150g unsalted butter, softened
50g caster sugar
300g full fat cream cheese

FOR THE DECORATION
edible flowers and leaves, e.g.
   nasturtiums, rose petals, lemon balm
   leaves, mint leaves, borage flowers

JUSTIN'S GINGER CAKE

Dark, rich, spicy and moist, this is one of my best recipes and probably the best ginger cake in the world, if I do say so myself. You can ice it and serve it as a celebratory cake, but it is also great as a dessert — serve it warm, with cider and caramel sauce and some vanilla ice cream.

First sift the flour and ground spices into a large bowl. Pour the milk into a large, heavy-based saucepan, add the sugar and let it dissolve over a medium heat, stirring frequently. As soon as it's at scalding point, remove from the heat and add the bicarbonate of soda: watch out, it will fizz up a little. Leave to one side for 10 minutes.

Put the butter, black treacle and golden syrup into a medium saucepan, place on a medium heat and slowly bring up to a light simmer, until the ingredients have melted and formed a rich syrup. Whisk this mixture into the flour little by little; it will be quite firm to start with but once about half of it is in it will be a bit lighter on the whisk. Then gradually whisk in the milk mixture, until smooth. If it's not smooth, pass the mixture through a sieve. Add the stem ginger pieces, ginger syrup and egg, give it a good whisk, then cover the bowl and leave to rest at room temperature for 2 hours.

Preheat the oven to 160°C/fan 140°C/gas 3. Lightly grease a 26cm springform cake tin and line the base and sides with baking paper. Give the cake mixture a good stir and pour it into the prepared tin. Bake for about 1 hour, until firm to the touch.

Meanwhile make the cider and caramel sauce. Put the apple juice and cider into a large, heavy-based saucepan and bring to the boil, then reduce the heat and simmer until reduced by one-third.

Put the sugar, lemon juice and 25ml of water into another large, heavy-based saucepan. Heat the mixture slowly to dissolve the sugar, stirring, then bring to the boil and cook over a medium heat until the mixture caramelizes to a dark golden colour. Add the reduced cider/apple juice (this stops the caramel from going any darker) and whisk in the butter. Mix in the cornflour with 15ml of water. Bring the cider mix up to a simmer and whisk in the cornflour mix. Simmer until thickened, then take off the heat and leave for 5–10 minutes to thicken a bit more.

When the cake is ready, leave it to cool in the tin for 20 minutes, then turn out and either place on a rack to cool completely or serve straight away, with the warm cider and caramel sauce and vanilla ice cream.

Serves 12–14
Suitable for freezing (although the sponge also keeps well in an airtight box)
Preparation time: 20 minutes
Resting time: 2 hours
Cooking time: 1 hour

300g self-raising flour
2 tablespoons ground ginger
1 teaspoon ground cinnamon
1 teaspoon ground mixed spice
375ml full fat milk
165g soft dark brown sugar
1 teaspoon bicarbonate of soda
150g unsalted butter, diced, plus extra for greasing
85g black treacle
165g golden syrup
65g stem ginger, chopped
80g stem syrup from the ginger jar
1 egg, beaten

FOR THE CIDER AND CARAMEL SAUCE
125ml apple juice
500ml cider
100g granulated sugar
juice of 1 lemon
55g butter, softened
15g cornflour

CHOCOLATE MOUSSE CAKE

This is more of a pudding than a cake, although it sits well in both camps, using the same mix but different cooking times to produce two layers of textures, the bottom being more of a cake and the top layer like a just-set mousse.

Serves 10–12
Not suitable for freezing
Preparation time: 25 minutes
Cooking time: 50 minutes

11 eggs
360g caster sugar
360g unsalted butter, diced
360g dark chocolate (70%), chopped or buttons
125g cocoa powder
½ teaspoon fine sea salt
crème fraîche, to serve

Preheat the oven to 160°C/fan 140°C/gas 3. Lightly grease a 26cm springform cake tin and line the base and sides with baking paper.

Separate your eggs, putting the yolks into the bowl of an electric mixer with the sugar, and the whites into a large metal or glass bowl.

Put the diced butter and the chocolate into a large heatproof bowl and place it over a pan of lightly simmering water, whisking from time to time until melted.

Whisk the egg yolks and sugar until light and fluffy (around 4 minutes), then turn off the mixer and sift in the cocoa powder. Turn the machine on again to a low speed and mix until the cocoa is incorporated, then turn it off and transfer the mixture into a large mixing bowl. Whisk in the melted chocolate and salt.

Use a hand mixer to whisk up the egg whites until they reach stiff peaks, then fold them into the chocolate mixture – it's easiest to do this in stages, a third first, then the rest.

Pour two-thirds of the mixture into your prepared cake tin and bake for 30 minutes. Take the cake out of the oven and let it cool for 20 minutes, then pour the rest of the mix into the tin on top of the baked mix. Smooth the top with a palette knife and return the cake to the oven for 20 minutes. Then remove and place on a rack to cool, still in the tin. Once completely cool, put it into the fridge for 4 hours or overnight, to set. Unmould an hour or two before serving to let it soften slightly.

Using a hot knife (place the blade under running hot water) will make it easy to cut into thin, even slices. Serve with a dollop of crème fraîche.

EARL GREY AND HONEY LOAF

First make the tea by putting the tea or teabags into a large bowl and pouring over the boiling water. Add the raisins and honey, mix well, then cover and leave overnight.

The next day, preheat the oven to 160°C/fan 140°C/gas 3 and grease and line a 900g loaf tin.

Most of the liquid will have been absorbed by the fruit by now. Take out the teabags or muslin bag of tea leaves and squeeze over the fruit, then discard. Add the sifted flour, lemon zest, sugars, beaten egg and milk to the soaked fruit, and mix together. Spoon into the tin and level the top with the back of the spoon. Bake for 55 minutes to 1 hour. The cake is ready when it is golden brown, firm to the touch and a skewer comes out clean.

Remove from the oven and leave to cool in the tin for 10 minutes before turning out.

Serve warm, in slices, with lots of salted butter.

Makes about 10 slices
Not suitable for freezing
Preparation time: 15 minutes
Marinating time: overnight
Cooking time: 1 hour

160ml Earl Grey tea (made with about 1 tablespoon of loose tea, wrapped in muslin, or 2 Earl Grey teabags)
225g raisins
2 tablespoons clear honey
225g self-raising flour, sifted
zest of 1 lemon
60g caster sugar
60g demerara sugar
1 egg, beaten
45ml full fat milk

CROQUEMBOUCHE

Translating as 'crunch in the mouth', croquembouche is a traditional French dessert made with choux buns and caramel. I have been travelling around the country making bouches for about four years now, mostly for weddings, although I also made one at Claridge's, which was great fun. They are very impressive and theatrical, as tradition calls for the bride and groom to smash the bouche (I've seen them smashed with rolling pins, a cricket bat, swords – even a baseball bat). This recipe is for a small croquembouche but you can increase the quantities to make a larger one. It takes a fair bit of time and some skill, but do give it a try.

The largest croquembouche I have made used 800 profiteroles and lots of caramel, and involved a few burnt fingers...

If you are going to use a nougatine base, make it first. You have to work quickly, as once you start to roll it out it begins to cool and will go very brittle.

Preheat the oven to 180°C/fan 160°C/gas 4 and line a baking tray with baking paper. Grease a 26cm flan ring (or use the outside of a 26cm springform cake tin). Place the flaked almonds in a small roasting tin and toast in the oven for about 12–15 minutes, until golden brown, shaking occasionally to brown them evenly. Put to one side to cool completely.

Put the sugar into a large, heavy-based saucepan on a low heat. Let it melt, then cook until a pale golden caramel is reached. Stir in the almonds, then add the butter and mix until all is incorporated.

Pour the mixture on to the prepared baking tray, then lay another sheet of baking paper on top and start to roll it out. Roll it to 5mm thick, then press it with the back of a spoon into the prepared flan ring. Trim off the excess and leave to cool.

Put the trimmings back into a low oven to soften up again, then re-roll and cut into shapes for decoration.

Now make your profiteroles. Preheat the oven to 200°C/fan 180°C/gas 6 and line a large baking tray with baking paper.

Put the butter, water and sugar into a heavy-based saucepan and place over a medium heat until the butter has melted. Turn up the heat and bring to the boil. Take off the heat and stir in the sifted flour and salt. Put back on the heat and cook for about 2–3 minutes, until the paste leaves the sides of the pan. Take off the heat and leave to cool completely.

»

Makes 60 profiteroles
Not suitable for freezing
Preparation time: 60 minutes
Cooking time: 1 hour 30 minutes

FOR THE NOUGATINE BASE (OPTIONAL)
125g flaked almonds
170g caster sugar
15g unsalted butter

FOR THE PROFITEROLES
500ml water
200g unsalted butter
10g caster sugar
280g strong white bread flour, sifted
a pinch of fine sea salt
8 eggs

FOR THE FILLING
double quantity of the crème patissière recipe (see page 146)

FOR THE CARAMEL
1kg granulated sugar
130ml liquid glucose
230ml water

Using a wooden spoon, beat in the eggs one at a time, waiting until each is completely mixed in before adding the next one, until they're all incorporated and the mixture is glossy and smooth. Using a large piping bag fitted with a 1.5–2cm plain nozzle, and working in four batches, pipe the mixture on to the prepared baking tray in 3cm rounds (if they have a little peak, press it down with a damp finger), leaving some room between as they will spread a little. You should be able to make 55–60 profiteroles from this amount of mixture. Leave the raw mix in the piping bag until each batch is going into the oven. They need to be cooked on the top shelf, so don't bake more than one batch at a time (unless you have more than one oven).

Bake for 20 minutes, or until risen and golden brown. Do not open the oven at all while they're baking, otherwise they won't rise as well. When ready, take out of the oven and place immediately on a cooling rack.

Once the profiteroles are cold, make a hole using a skewer or small kitchen knife in the bottom of each one and pipe in your crème patissière, using a large piping bag and a 7–8mm nozzle. The profiteroles must be filled and eaten on the day they're made – if stored the pastry goes soft very quickly.

To make the caramel, put all the ingredients into a very clean heavy-based saucepan on a low heat. Once the sugar and glucose have melted, turn the heat up to high and bring the temperature to 160°C on a digital thermometer (making sure the reading is from the middle of the caramel and not the bottom of the saucepan). Once the temperature is reached, put the saucepan into a cold water bath in the sink for 1–2 minutes to stop the caramel colouring any further (watch out as you put the saucepan into the water bath as it will spit boiling water around).

Wearing gloves to protect your hands, dip each of your profiteroles top down into the caramel and lay each one on a lined baking tray, caramel side down. Leave to cool and set. If the caramel in the pan starts to harden, simply heat it gently to liquefy it again.

Now to assemble your croquembouche. On a serving tray, or your nougatine base if you have made one, dip each of the profiteroles into the caramel on the side and start to build the bouche. The top of the profiterole becomes the side facing out, so you have a lovely shiny outside. Keep stacking them up and dipping them into the caramel until you have a pyramid shape. As before, if the caramel in the pan starts to harden, just put it back on a low heat until softened again.

You can decorate the croquembouche with nougatine shapes, gold and silver leaf, sugared almonds, raspberries and sugar flowers (check out the picture opposite for more ideas).

To serve, smash the bouche with a rolling pin and serve with pouring cream.

WELSH CAKES

These are traditionally baked on a bakestone, but a heavy-based frying pan is fine too. Make sure you eat the cakes straight from the pan – a great teatime treat.

Put the flour, salt and butter into a large bowl and rub together until it looks like breadcrumbs. Add the mixed spice, sultanas and sugars and mix together well, then add the honey, followed by the beaten egg.

Mix until all is combined, then bring together to form a dough. Wrap it in clingfilm and put it into the fridge to rest for 1 hour.

On a lightly floured surface, roll out the dough to 1cm thick. Using a 6cm round cutter, cut out 12 rounds, re-rolling when necessary, and put them on a lightly floured baking tray.

Heat a large (26cm), heavy-based non-stick frying pan on a medium heat and put half the Welsh cakes in, making sure you don't overcrowd the frying pan. No oil or fat is needed, just dry heat. Lower the heat to the lowest setting and cook them on each side for 4–5 minutes, until dark golden brown, taking care they don't catch and burn. Cook the second batch the same way.

Serve straight from the frying pan, either just as they are or with plenty of butter. They can also be kept for a few days and reheated in the oven for a few minutes at 180°C/fan 160°C/gas 4.

Makes 12
Suitable for freezing
Preparation time: 15 minutes
Resting time: 1 hour
Cooking time: 20 minutes

225g self-raising flour, sifted, plus extra for dusting
a pinch of fine sea salt
125g unsalted butter, cubed
½ teaspoon mixed spice
125g sultanas
15g demerara sugar
80g caster sugar
1 tablespoon clear honey
1 egg, beaten

HOT CROSS BUNS

These are an Easter classic, but you can make them during the rest of the year without the cross and have lovely spiced fruit buns for tea. You can also roll the dough into two logs and bake it in two 450g loaf tins, to make loaves instead of buns or, if you have any left over, use it to make a cheeky bread and butter pudding.

STAGE 1: Put the flour, sugar, spices and zest into the bowl of an electric mixer with a hook attachment and add 300g of water. In a jug or bowl, whisk together the black treacle, yeast and water and add to the dry ingredients. Mix for 4 minutes on medium speed, then cover the bowl and leave for 1 hour.

STAGE 2: Add the stage 2 ingredients to the stage 1 mix, and mix together on a medium speed until all is incorporated.

STAGE 3: Add the stage 3 ingredients to the stage 1 and 2 mix and mix together on a medium speed until you have a glossy, smooth dough (it will be fairly sticky). If the dough seems too wet, add a little more flour. Then cover the bowl and leave somewhere warm for 2 hours.

Line a baking tray with baking paper. Place the mixture on a lightly floured surface and cut into 120g pieces. Roll the pieces into balls and place them on the prepared baking tray, leaving plenty of room between them as they will spread out. Cover with clingfilm and set aside until doubled in size (this should take about 1 hour).

While the buns are proving, make the cross mix and the glaze.

To make the cross mix, whisk the sifted flour, sugar, salt and 120g of water together until you have a smooth paste and pour it into a piping bag with a 4mm wide plain nozzle.

For the glaze, place the sugar and glucose in a heavy-based saucepan with 100g of water, bring to the boil, then reduce the heat and simmer until the temperature reaches 105°C on a kitchen thermometer – it will take about 5 minutes.

Preheat the oven to 180°C/fan 160°C/gas 4.

Once the buns have proved, pipe a cross on top of each one and bake for 14–15 minutes, until golden brown. Remove from the oven and place on a cooling rack. After 2 minutes, brush with the bun glaze. Serve warm, with plenty of butter.

Makes 14
Suitable for freezing (as raw dough or cooked buns)
Preparation time: 25 minutes
Proving/resting time: 4 hours
Cooking time: 15 minutes

STAGE 1

225g strong white bread flour
70g dark brown sugar
1 teaspoon ground mixed spice
1 teaspoon ground ginger
½ teaspoon ground cinnamon
zest of 2 oranges
30g black treacle
25g fresh yeast, crumbled

STAGE 2

400g strong white bread flour
2 egg yolks
1½ teaspoons fine sea salt
125g softened unsalted butter, chopped small

STAGE 3

125g chopped mixed peel
4 pieces of stem ginger, chopped small
1 tablespoon syrup from the ginger jar
250g raisins

FOR THE CROSS

100g strong white bread flour
a pinch of caster sugar
a pinch of fine sea salt

FOR THE GLAZE

100g caster sugar
20ml liquid glucose

BOMBER COMMAND BUNS

These buns came about when Henrietta Lovell of the Rare Tea Company (rareteacompany.com) asked me to make some buns for the unveiling of the memorial to Bomber Command in Green Park on 4 July 2012.

I was honoured to help, and we made about 1,500 of these buns, although Henrietta made 4,000 cups of 'Royal Air Force' tea on the day.

Line a baking tray with baking paper.

Put the flour, salt, sugar, orange and lemon zest, raisins and currants into the bowl of an electric mixer and mix well to combine. Put 300ml of water into a jug or bowl, then add the yeast and whisk until dissolved.

Pour the yeast liquid into the mixer bowl and, using a dough hook attachment, mix on a medium speed for 6–8 minutes, or until it starts coming away from the sides. Add the remaining 30ml of water as needed, if the dough looks dry (you may not need any). Turn off the mixer and let the dough rest for 10 minutes.

Start the mixer up again on a medium speed and slowly add the butter to the dough, a teaspoon at a time (this should take about 5 minutes). Once the butter is incorporated, mix on high speed for 1 minute, then cover the bowl with clingfilm and let it rest for 10 minutes.

Tip the dough out on to a lightly floured surface and knead together lightly and briefly. Divide it into 40g pieces and roll them into balls, then place them on the prepared baking tray and cover with a clean tea-towel or lightly with clingfilm. Leave to prove until doubled in size (about 1 hour).

Preheat the oven to 200°C/fan 180°C/gas 6.

Brush the tops of the buns with the beaten egg and bake for about 10–12 minutes, or until golden brown.

Eat them plain or with butter and jam.

Makes about 32
Suitable for freezing (raw dough or
    cooked buns)
Preparation time: 25 minutes
Proving/resting time: 1 hour 20 minutes
Cooking time: 12 minutes

600g strong white bread flour,
    plus extra for dusting
12g fine sea salt
60g caster sugar
zest of 2 oranges
zest of 1 lemon
50g raisins
50g currrants
300–330g water
22g fresh yeast, crumbled
125g softened unsalted butter
1 egg, beaten, to glaze

DEVONSHIRE SPLITS

A fantastic alternative to scones, these enriched little bread buns are light and delicious, and they're not just for serving with cream and jam – try a ball of ice cream in them instead. They do need to be served warm and on the day they're made, though they also freeze well.

Sift the flour, salt and sugar into a large bowl and mix well. Put the milk, crumbled yeast and melted butter into a jug or bowl and whisk to combine well and dissolve the yeast. Add the milk mixture to the dry ingredients and mix to form a dough.

Transfer to a lightly floured surface and knead by hand for 2 minutes. Put back into a lightly floured bowl, cover and place in a warm place for 1–1½ hours, until doubled in size.

Line two baking trays with baking paper. Divide the dough into 12 equal pieces and roll each one into a ball. Put them on the prepared baking trays, leaving room between them as they will spread. Sprinkle with flour, then cover and leave in a warm place for about 1 hour, or until they have doubled in size.

Preheat the oven to 200°C/fan 180°C/gas 6. Bake the buns for 15 minutes, until golden brown, then place on a rack and leave to cool.

To serve, split them (but not all the way through), fill them with extra thick Jersey cream and top with jam.

Makes 12
Perfect for freezing
Preparation time: 15 minutes
Proving time: 2–2½ hours
Cooking time: 15 minutes

450g plain flour, plus extra
    for dusting
½ teaspoon fine sea salt
1 teaspoon caster sugar
275ml full fat milk
15g fresh yeast, crumbled
50g unsalted butter, melted

TO SERVE
thick Jersey cream
jam (the raspberry jam on
    page 241 is perfect)

ICED LONDON BUNS

A fairly forgotten treat, these teatime buns are fragrant with orange and caraway and delicious any time. Don't be scared of the caraway in this recipe – it really does work.

Line a baking tray with baking paper. Put the flour, salt, sugar, peel, orange zest and caraway seeds into the bowl of an electric mixer. Put 150g of water into a bowl or jug and add the yeast. When it has dissolved, add to the flour, then mix on a medium speed for 8 minutes, or until the mixture starts coming away from the sides. Turn off the mixer and let the dough rest for 5 minutes.

Start the mixer up again on a medium speed and slowly add the butter a teaspoon at a time, only adding the next piece once the previous butter is completely incorporated. Once all the butter is in, mix on high speed for 1 minute. Cover the bowl with clingfilm and let it rest for 10 minutes. Divide the dough into 12 pieces and roll them into fat sausage shapes about 8–9cm in length. Place them on the prepared baking tray, cover lightly, and leave for about 1½ hours, until doubled in size.

Preheat the oven to 200°C/fan 180°C/gas 6. Eggwash the buns and bake for about 10–12 minutes, or until golden brown.

To make the icing, put the glucose and lemon juice into a heatproof bowl and place over a pan of simmering water to gently melt the glucose. Sift in the icing sugar and whisk together until smooth, removing the bowl when the icing starts to warm up. Pour the icing into a piping bag and leave for a few minutes.

Once the buns are cold, pipe the icing on top, along the centre of each bun.

Makes 12
Suitable for freezing (un-iced)
Preparation time: 25 minutes
Proving time: 1 hour 45 minutes
Cooking time: 12 minutes

300g strong white bread flour,
    plus extra for dusting
1 teaspoon fine sea salt
35g caster sugar
50g chopped candied peel
zest of 1 orange
1½ teaspoons caraway seeds
150–180g water
10g fresh yeast, crumbled
75g softened unsalted butter
1 egg, beaten, to glaze

FOR THE ICING
40ml liquid glucose
40ml lemon juice
300g icing sugar

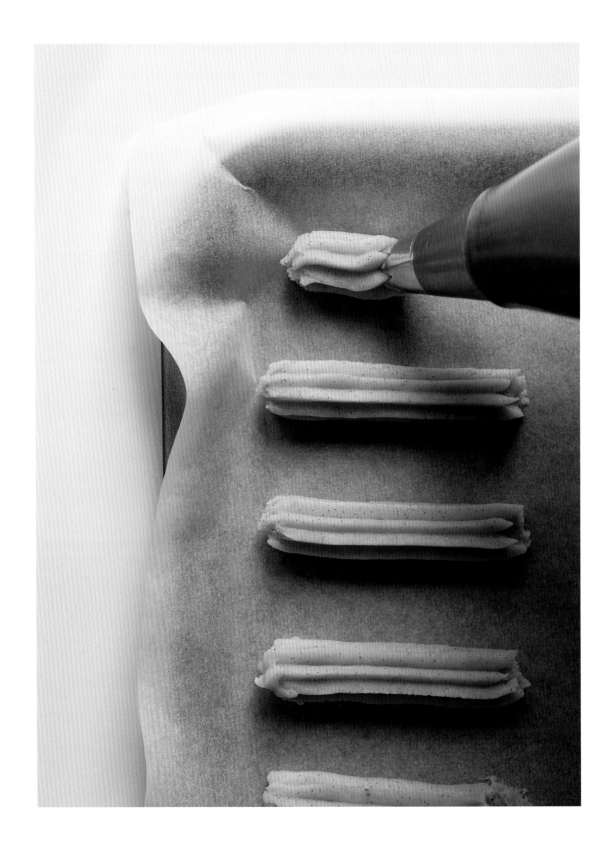

BISCUITS

I grew up with all the classic biscuits like jammy dodgers, ginger nuts and custard creams, but as a pastry chef I really wanted to add something to these traditional recipes by making them richer and more luxurious.

The great thing about biscuits is that you can eat them any time of day – with your first cuppa in the morning, with desserts like ice cream and creamy puddings, as petits fours with coffee, or even as a cheesecake base.

The quantities in these biscuit recipes are fairly large, the reason being that they freeze really well uncooked and ready-portioned, making them perfect for taking out of the freezer to bake when friends and family are around.

For making biscuits you need a couple of good flat baking trays, lots of different size cutters (note that if you are using a different size to what's stated in the recipe you will have to adjust the cooking times accordingly). A silicon mat is quite useful too, as baking paper can fly around a bit in the oven.

Most of these biscuit recipes are simple to make – so stop buying them and start making them.

CHOCOLATE AND OAT SNAPS

These biscuits are a bit like brandy snaps but are more delicate and fragile – absolutely delicious. A really good biscuit to serve with ice cream and creamy desserts. They're also ideal for gluten/wheat-free diets. The mix keeps well in the fridge for a couple of weeks.

Makes about 28
Not suitable for freezing
Preparation time: 15 minutes,
    plus chilling time
Cooking time: 20 minutes

125g dark chocolate (70%),
    chopped, or buttons
125g softened unsalted butter
110g caster sugar
85g soft light brown sugar
1 egg
½ teaspoon vanilla extract
90g jumbo oats
a pinch of fine sea salt
½ teaspoon baking powder
½ teaspoon bicarbonate of soda

First cut your chocolate into small pieces if you are not using chocolate buttons.

In an electric mixer with a beater attachment, or in a bowl with a wooden spoon, cream the butter and both sugars together until light and fluffy. Add the egg a little at a time, beating as you go, until incorporated, then add the rest of the ingredients and mix together. Put the mix into the fridge for a few hours, until firm.

Preheat the oven to 140°C/fan 120°C/gas 1 and line a baking tray with baking paper.

When the dough is firm, take it out of the fridge and roll it into balls about 20g in weight. Place them on the prepared baking tray, making sure you leave plenty of room (about 12cm) between them as they will spread out a lot (don't cook more than 6 or 7 at a time), and bake for 20 minutes.

Leave to cool on the tray, as they will be too fragile to move straight away.

Great served with ice cream.

DIGESTIVES

These are quite different from shop-bought digestives – they're not so sweet, and the coarse oatmeal brings a lovely texture and depth of flavour. You can reduce the sugar by half to make a delicious biscuit for cheese.

Cut your cold butter into small dice and put it into a bowl with the wholemeal flour, oatmeal, salt and sugar. Rub the mixture using your fingertips until it resembles fine breadcrumbs. Mix the vinegar, milk and bicarbonate of soda in a small jug or bowl, add to the bowl of dry ingredients and mix until you have a workable dough. Wrap in clingfilm and chill in the fridge for at least 2 hours.

Preheat the oven to 140°C/fan 120°C/gas 1 and line two baking trays with baking paper.

Take the dough out of the fridge and let it soften a little, then roll it out on a floured surface to 5mm thick. Using an 8cm cutter, cut out rounds and place them on the prepared baking trays. Re-roll the dough and cut out more, to make 25 biscuits in total. Bake for 22 minutes, or until golden brown.

Leave them to cool on the trays.

Really good with a mug of tea or to use as a cheesecake base.

Makes about 25
Suitable for freezing (uncooked dough or cooked biscuits)
Preparation time: 20 minutes, plus chilling time
Cooking time: 22 minutes

165g cold unsalted butter
225g plain wholemeal flour
225g coarse or medium oatmeal
1/4 teaspoon fine sea salt
80g soft light brown sugar
1 teaspoon white wine vinegar
100ml full fat milk
1 teaspoon bicarbonate of soda

GINGER NUTS

One of my favourite biscuits, with a strong punch of spicing and a really good crunch. They make a cheeky cheesecake base, or you can crunch them up and fold the pieces through freshly churned vanilla ice cream.

Cut the stem ginger into small pieces. Sift the flour, bicarbonate of soda and spices into a mixing bowl, then add the rest of the ingredients and mix well (best to use an electric mixer for this one). Put the dough on a lightly floured surface and bring it together, then shape into a flattened ball. Wrap in clingfilm and put into the fridge to chill for a few hours.

Preheat the oven to 160°C/fan 140°C/gas 3 and line two large baking trays with baking paper.

Roll the dough into 25g balls and place them on the prepared baking trays, pressing each ball down lightly with the palm of your hand. Make sure you leave plenty of room between them, as they will spread. They will need to be cooked in four batches, but you can just re-use the prepared trays, allowing them to cool first. Bake for 20–22 minutes.

Leave to cool on the trays.

Makes about 50
Suitable for freezing (uncooked dough or cooked biscuits)
Preparation time: 20 minutes, plus chilling time
Cooking time: 22 minutes

150g stem ginger
500g self-raising flour, plus extra for dusting
2 teaspoons bicarbonate of soda
2 teaspoons ground mixed spice
1 teaspoon ground cinnamon
6 teaspoons ground ginger
1 teaspoon ground allspice
150g soft dark brown sugar
250g softened unsalted butter
250g golden syrup

THE PERFECT DUNKING BISCUIT

I've always loved to dunk biscuits in my tea, but most of the time they fall apart, so I've developed the perfect recipe. These are the best biscuits to use for dunking, as the flavour of golden syrup and honey is released into the tea and they hold a good few dunks.

Preheat the oven to 180°C/fan 160°C/gas 4 and line a baking tray with baking paper.

Mix the oats and icing sugar together in a small bowl and put them on to the prepared baking tray, spreading them evenly in one layer. Toast them for 12–14 minutes, stirring every few minutes or until evenly golden brown, then leave until cold.

Cut the butter into small pieces and combine with all the remaining ingredients in the bowl of an electric mixer with a beater attachment, or in a bowl with a wooden spoon, until the mix forms a ball. Put into the fridge to chill for a couple of hours.

Take the dough out of the fridge and leave it to soften for about 2–3 hours.

Preheat the oven to 140°C/fan 120°C/gas 1 and line two large baking trays with baking paper.

On a lightly floured surface, roll out your mix to 5mm thick and cut into rectangles about 3cm by 6cm. Place them on the prepared baking trays and bake for 15 minutes, or until golden brown.

Leave them on the trays for 5 minutes, then put them on a rack to cool.

Serve with a mug of tea, or coffee, if you must.

Makes about 30–40

Suitable for freezing (uncooked dough or cooked biscuits)

Preparation time: 20 minutes, plus chilling time

Cooking time: 30 minutes

75g jumbo oats

15g icing sugar

175g softened unsalted butter

175g soft light brown sugar

340g plain flour, plus extra for dusting

2 teaspoons baking powder

60g golden syrup

20g runny honey

1½ tablespoons full fat milk

THE MEGA MILKY MALT

I was given a mega mug, so I had to make a mega biscuit … I knew it had to have milk and malt in it, and so it was born, the big daddy of biscuits: the MEGA MILKY MALTY BISCUIT for your mega mug.

In an electric mixer with a beater attachment, or in a bowl with a wooden spoon, cream your butter and sugars together until light and fluffy. Add the eggs gradually, stirring all the time, then mix in the two syrups followed by the milk powder. Finally add the sifted flour and salt and mix until all is incorporated.

Place in a bowl, cover with clingfilm and chill overnight in the fridge.

Preheat the oven to 150°C/fan 130°C/gas 2 and line a baking tray with baking paper.

On a lightly floured surface, roll out the dough to 5mm thick. Using a 10cm cutter, cut out your biscuits and place them on the prepared baking tray, making sure you leave plenty of room between them as they will spread. Bake for 16–18 minutes, until golden brown and baked through.

Leave them on the tray for 5 minutes, then put them on a rack to cool. Serve with a mega mug of tea or coffee.

Makes 22

Suitable for freezing (uncooked dough or cooked biscuits)

Preparation time: 20 minutes, plus chilling time

Cooking time: 16 minutes

250g softened unsalted butter
125g caster sugar
125g soft light brown sugar
2 eggs, beaten
2 tablespoons malt syrup
1 tablespoon golden syrup
50g milk powder, sieved
400g plain flour, sifted, plus extra for dusting
a pinch of fine sea salt

JAMMY DODGERS

The classic. You can use a different jam if you like, but I do think the raspberry jam from the store cupboard chapter is the one, and makes these really special.

Put all the ingredients apart from the filling into a food processor and whiz until a ball of dough is formed. Wrap it in clingfilm and put it into the fridge to chill.

Preheat the oven to 160°C/fan 140°C/gas 3 and line two large baking trays with baking paper.

Take the dough out of the fridge and leave for an hour to soften. On a lightly floured surface, roll it out to 3–4 mm thick, then, using a 6cm cutter, cut out your rounds to make the bases. To make the tops, take half the rounds and cut out the centre, using a 2cm cutter. Keep rolling and cutting until you have 20 bases and 20 tops.

Place the biscuits without a hole on the prepared baking trays and put ½ teaspoon of the jam of your choice in the centre, spreading it out slightly. Place the biscuits with the holes on top, pressing slightly so the jam rises out from the centre a little. Put into the fridge to chill for 5 minutes, then bake for 20–22 minutes, or until lightly golden brown.

Sprinkle the biscuits immediately with the caster sugar. Leave on the trays for 5 minutes, then put them on a rack to cool.

Makes about 18–20
Suitable for freezing
   (uncooked dough)
Preparation time: 20 minutes,
   plus chilling time
Cooking time: 20 minutes

250g plain flour, plus extra
   for dusting
110g icing sugar
200g softened unsalted butter
2 egg yolks
a pinch of fine sea salt

FOR THE FILLING
130g raspberry jam
   (see page 241)
2 teaspoons caster sugar,
   for sprinkling

BROWN SUGAR AND PRUNE ROLLS

My version of the fig roll. These are a bit heavier and more filling than most of the biscuit recipes, and they also make a lovely dessert, served warm with vanilla ice cream.

First make the filling. Put the prunes into a small bowl. Bring the water and sugar to the boil and pour over the prunes, then leave for a few hours to stand, stirring a couple of times. Put them into a food processor and whiz to make a purée, then place the purée in a bowl and mix in the crumbs. Put into the fridge for 1 hour, to firm up.

Put the flour into a bowl. Dice the butter and add to the bowl, then rub together until the mixture looks like fine crumbs. Add the rest of the pastry ingredients and mix until you have a smooth paste. Wrap in clingfilm and put into the fridge to chill for a few hours.

Preheat the oven to 160°C/fan 140°C/gas 3 and line two large baking trays with baking paper.

Divide your prune filling into three sections and roll them into log shapes with the help of some icing sugar – they will need to be about 30cm long. Put the logs into the fridge again, just while the pastry is being rolled.

Remove the clingfilm from the pastry and knead it until it is ready to roll. On a lightly floured surface, roll it into a rectangle about 27cm x 32cm, then cut lengthways into three strips, each 9cm wide.

Place the strips on the work surface with the short ends towards you, and lay the prune logs down the centre. Using a pastry brush or your finger, wet the edges of the pastry with water and wrap the pastry over the filling to meet the other side, overlapping the edges a little and sealing them together.

Gently press them down so they are halved in height. Trim the ends, then cut them into 3cm rolls and place on the prepared baking trays, making sure the seal is underneath. Put into the fridge to chill for 15 minutes, then bake for about 18–20 minutes, or until golden brown.

Leave on the trays for a few minutes, then put them on a rack to cool.

Makes 30

Suitable for freezing (uncooked dough or rolls)

Preparation time: 30 minutes, plus chilling time

Cooking time: 20 minutes

FOR THE FILLING

300g dried stoned pitted prunes

75ml water

25g soft dark brown sugar

30g cake crumbs or breadcrumbs

icing sugar, for dusting

FOR THE PASTRY

260g plain flour, plus extra for dusting

125g cold unsalted butter

50g soft light brown sugar

25g dark brown sugar

1 tablespoon black treacle

1 egg

¾ teaspoon baking powder

a pinch of fine sea salt

CUSTARD CREAMS

These are more luxurious than the traditional custard creams, with a melt-in-the-mouth texture and a rich, velvety custard filling.

Split the vanilla pod lengthways and scrape out the seeds, keeping half back for the filling. Put the other half of the seeds into a food processor with the flour, icing sugar, butter, egg yolk and salt, and whiz until a ball of dough is formed. Wrap in clingfilm, then put into the fridge to chill for 2–3 hours.

Make the filling by mixing the butter and the other half of the vanilla seeds together in a bowl until fluffy. Add the sifted icing sugar and mix until smooth and creamy, beating for about 2 minutes.

Take the dough out of the fridge and leave for an hour to soften.

Preheat the oven to 140°C/fan 120°C/gas 1 and line two large baking trays with baking paper.

Roll out the dough to 3–4 mm thick, then cut by hand into rectangles 4cm x 5cm.

Place all the rectangles on the prepared baking trays and chill for 5 minutes in the fridge, then bake for 20 minutes, or until golden brown. Sprinkle half the biscuits with caster sugar and put them all on a rack to cool, then sandwich in pairs with the custard mix, using the biscuits sprinkled with sugar on top.

Makes 15
Suitable for freezing
   (uncooked dough)
Preparation time: 20 minutes,
   plus chilling time
Cooking time: 20 minutes

½ a vanilla pod
125g plain flour, plus extra
   for dusting
55g icing sugar
100g softened unsalted butter
1 egg yolk
a pinch of fine sea salt
2 teaspoons caster sugar,
   for sprinkling

FOR THE FILLING
80g softened unsalted butter
the other ½ of the vanilla pod
150g icing sugar, sifted

COCONUT AND CARDAMOM BISCUITS

I first tried a biscuit similar to this in Goa, in India, and when I got home I came up with this recipe. The spicing of cardamom is fairly strong, so feel free to cut it down to your taste (start with half a teaspoon). If you like cardamom, however, you will really love these. Lovely to eat as petits fours with your coffee after a dinner party.

Take the cardamom seeds out of their pods and grind them in a spice grinder with 1 tablespoon of the caster sugar until they make a fine powder. You need about 2 teaspoons of ground cardamom.

Put the butter, remaining caster sugar, demerara, flour, eggs, coconut and ground cardamom into a food processor and mix together until everything is incorporated and forms a paste. Scrape out and wrap in clingfilm. Put into the fridge to chill for a few hours.

Preheat the oven to 140°C/fan 120°C/gas 1 and line a baking tray with baking paper.

Roll the mix into balls of about 12g each and toss them in icing sugar, then put them on the prepared baking tray and press them down flat, using a fork. Bake for 20 minutes.

Best served warm.

Makes about 50 small biscuits
Suitable for freezing (uncooked dough or cooked biscuits)
Preparation time: 25 minutes, plus chilling time
Cooking time: 20 minutes

2 tablespoons cardamom pods
100g caster sugar
80g softened butter
60g demerara sugar
180g plain flour
2 eggs, beaten
140g desiccated coconut
75g icing sugar, for dusting

Left, top to bottom: the nutter, jammy dodger
Middle: mega milky malt
Right, top to bottom: very orange biscuit, coconut and cardamom biscuit

THE NUTTER

These were inspired by that bowl of nuts you always have at Christmas that are still sitting there in the spring, and all those half-opened packets of nuts that sit at the back of the store cupboard. You can use any type of nuts – just keep the quantity the same in total. These are great served with chocolate pots (see page 199).

Makes about 25
Suitable for freezing (uncooked dough or cooked biscuits)
Preparation time: 20 minutes, plus chilling time
Cooking time: 25 minutes

50g blanched almonds
50g blanched hazelnuts
50g walnuts
50g Brazil nuts
50g macadamia nuts
125g softened unsalted butter
125g caster sugar
1 egg, beaten
150g plain flour, plus extra for dusting

Preheat the oven to 180°C/fan 160°C/gas 4.

Place all the nuts in a small roasting tin and roast for 12–14 minutes, until golden brown, stirring at least twice. Remove and leave to cool completely. Turn the oven off for now.

Whiz up the nuts in a food processor, or chop with a large kitchen knife, until they are small crumbs.

In an electric mixer with a beater attachment, or in a bowl with a wooden spoon, cream the butter and sugar together until light and fluffy. Add the egg gradually, making sure it's all incorporated, then add the flour and nuts and mix together, bringing the dough together into a ball. Wrap in clingfilm and put into the fridge to chill for a few hours.

Preheat the oven to 140°C/fan 120°C/gas 1 and line a baking tray with baking paper.

Take the dough out of the fridge and let it soften a little, but not too much, otherwise it will get sticky. On a lightly floured surface, roll out half the dough at a time to 5mm thick. Using a 7cm cutter, cut out rounds and place them on the prepared baking tray. Bake for 20–25 minutes, or until golden brown.

Leave them on the tray for 5 minutes, then put them on a rack to cool.

TUILES

Great to serve with ice cream or a mousse. You will need a stencil, which is easy to make out of a plastic lid (see the instructions below).

To make your stencil, get a plastic lid (something like an ice cream tub lid) and draw on it an outline of the desired shape (keep it simple and draw something like a square, triangle or circle). Then, using a pair of scissors, cut out the shape and trim the stencil to 2cm on each side (see opposite). When using the stencil for the tuiles, place it on the baking tray, spread the mixture into the stencil and scrape any excess away across the top. Then lift up the stencil and use it again until the baking sheet is full.

Sift your flour and icing sugar into a bowl, then transfer to a food processor, add the cooled melted butter and the egg whites, and whiz until smooth (it will be a bit runny). Put the mix into a container and place in the fridge to firm up for a few hours.

Preheat the oven to 160°C/fan 140°C/gas 3 and line a couple of baking trays with baking paper.

Once the mix is firm you can start: place your stencil on one of your prepared baking trays. Using a small palette knife, take a small amount of mix (about 20g) and spread it out evenly over the stencil. Put 6–8 tuiles on each tray (you will end up doing three batches).

Bake for about 11–12 minutes, or until they start to go golden brown – you will need to watch them like a hawk, as they burn very quickly.

When you take the tuiles out of the oven, remove them from the baking trays with a palette knife and shape each one over a rolling pin or an upturned bowl. Leave to cool completely. You can shape them into whatever your heart desires, but you need to act quickly, as when they cool they become brittle and easy to break.

Makes about 18 (depending on size and shape)
Suitable for freezing (uncooked dough or cooked tuiles, though the latter are very fragile)
Preparation time: 15 minutes, plus chilling time
Cooking time: 12 minutes

110g plain flour
175g icing sugar
110g melted butter (cooled to room temperature)
2 egg whites

VERY ORANGE BISCUITS

These have a really punchy orange flavour and a great crunch. Serve with any chocolate dessert.

Pour the orange juice into a saucepan and bring to the boil, then lower the heat and simmer until it has reduced to about 50ml of very thick and glossy juice (this should take about 10–15 minutes). Let it cool, then chill for at least a couple of hours.

In an electric mixer with a beater attachment, or in a bowl with a wooden spoon, cream the butter, sugars and orange zest together until light and fluffy, then beat in the egg. Add the flour, salt, baking powder and vanilla extract and beat together, and finally beat in the chilled reduced orange juice.

On a lightly floured surface, roll the dough into two logs about 25cm long, with a diameter of about 3cm. Wrap in clingfilm and put into the fridge to chill and harden for at least 3 hours.

Preheat the oven to 140°C/fan 120°C/gas 1 and line a baking tray with baking paper.

Once firm, slice the logs into rounds as thinly as you can – about 2mm is ideal (it might be a bit sticky). Place the rounds on the prepared baking tray and bake for 12–15 minutes, or until golden brown.

Sprinkle with caster sugar and put them on a rack to cool.

Makes about 25
Suitable for freezing (uncooked dough or cooked biscuits)
Preparation time: 20 minutes, plus chilling time
Cooking time: 30 minutes

juice and finely grated zest of 4 oranges
225g softened unsalted butter
125g caster sugar, plus extra for sprinkling
25g demerara sugar
75g soft light brown sugar
1 egg, beaten
300g plain flour, sifted
a pinch of fine sea salt
1¼ teaspoons baking powder
½ teaspoon vanilla extract

WHISKY AND SPICE
(AND ALL THINGS NICE)

My wife and I were in New Orleans on our honeymoon, in a speakeasy bar drinking amazing spiced whisky cocktails, and we both thought they would make great biscuits – so here they are.

Put the sultanas into a small bowl and pour over the whisky. Leave to soak overnight.

Preheat the oven to 160°C/fan 140°C/gas 3 and line two large baking trays with baking paper.

In an electric mixer with a beater attachment, or in a bowl with a wooden spoon, cream the butter and sugars together until light and fluffy. Add the egg yolks, one at a time, and mix in, then sift in the spices, flour, baking powder and salt and mix. Once all is incorporated, mix in the honey and finally fold in the soaked fruit, draining it first.

Spoon mounds of 2 teaspoonfuls of the mix at a time on to the prepared baking trays and bake for 25 minutes, or until golden brown.

Put them on a rack to cool.

Makes about 36
Suitable for freezing (cooked biscuits)
Preparation time: 15 minutes, plus overnight soaking
Cooking time: 25 minutes

170g sultanas
150ml whisky
100g butter
100g caster sugar
60g soft light brown sugar
2 egg yolks
½ teaspoon ground cloves
½ teaspoon ground nutmeg
½ teaspoon ground mace
½ teaspoon ground cinnamon
275g plain flour
½ teaspoon baking powder
a pinch of fine sea salt
2 tablespoons runny honey

BUTTER FINGERS

These are really rich buttery biscuits that are great for elevenses, or as petits fours to serve with coffee.

Preheat the oven to 160°C/fan 140°C/gas 3 and line two large baking trays with baking paper.

Sift the flour, salt and cornflour into a large bowl and mix together well.

Split the vanilla pod and scrape out the seeds. Put them into a food processor with the softened butter and icing sugar, then add the flour mix and whiz together until it becomes a smooth paste.

Put the mix into a piping bag with a 1cm wide star nozzle and pipe about 40 lines of fingers about 6cm long on to the prepared baking trays. Bake for 15 minutes, or until golden brown.

Leave on the trays for 5 minutes, then put on a rack to cool.

Melt the chocolate in a bowl over a pan of simmering water. When the fingers are cool, dip into your melted chocolate and place on a rack until the chocolate sets.

Makes about 40

Suitable for freezing
  (uncooked dough)

Preparation time: 25 minutes

Cooking time: 15 minutes

220g plain flour

a pinch of fine sea salt

70g cornflour

1 vanilla pod

250g softened unsalted butter

60g icing sugar

100g dark chocolate (70%),
  broken into pieces

GINGER SNAPS

You can serve these as biscuits, or you can use them to make ice cream baskets: let them cool a little, then place them on a upside-down espresso cup and mould them around it to make a basket shape. Leave to set, then fill them with balls of ice cream. The mix keeps well in the fridge for a month or two.

Put the butter, sugar, golden syrup and lemon juice into a heavy-based saucepan and melt together on a low heat, making sure the sugar has dissolved fully.

Sift the flour and ground ginger into a bowl and mix together, then add to the melted ingredients and stir. Pour into a plastic container and leave to get cold.

Preheat the oven to 160°C/fan 140°C/gas 3 and line two large baking trays with baking paper.

Once the dough is cold, roll it into small balls, about half the size of a walnut, and place on the prepared baking trays. The ginger snaps will spread, so make sure to leave plenty of room between them.

Bake for about 10 minutes, or until golden brown. The cooked snaps will be very flat and thin and will have a lacy appearance.

Leave them on the trays to cool, as they will be too fragile to move straight away.

Makes 36
Suitable for freezing (uncooked dough or cooked biscuits)
Preparation time: 20 minutes, plus cooling time
Cooking time: 10 minutes

100g unsalted butter, diced
100g light brown sugar
100g golden syrup
3 teaspoons lemon juice
100g plain flour
1 teaspoon ground ginger

PARMESAN OR CHEDDAR BISCUITS

Great to serve as a canapé with a glass of bubbles.

Put all the ingredients into a food processor and whiz together until the mixture forms a ball. Scrape out on to a piece of clingfilm and shape into a log 35cm long and 5cm in diameter. Wrap it in clingfilm and put into the fridge to chill for at least 2 hours, until firm.

Preheat the oven to 180°C/fan 160°C/gas 4 and line a baking tray with baking paper.

Remove the clingfilm and slice the log into rounds about 1cm thick. Place them on the prepared baking tray and bake for about 15 minutes, or until golden brown.

Leave on the tray for 5 minutes, then put them on a rack to cool.

Makes about 30–35

Suitable for freezing (uncooked dough or cooked biscuits)

Preparation time: 20 minutes, plus chilling time

Cooking time: 15 minutes

250g plain flour

250g grated Parmesan or strong Cheddar cheese – or half and half

250g softened unsalted butter

½ teaspoon ground cayenne pepper

1 teaspoon mustard powder

1 teaspoon fine sea salt

a good few twists of black pepper

OAT AND WHEAT BISCUITS

These melt in the mouth – you won't want to go back to a shop-bought oatcake after trying this delicious homemade version. Superb with blue cheese and chutney, or a tangy mature Cheddar.

Put all the ingredients apart from the water into a large bowl and rub the butter into the flour until the mix looks like breadcrumbs. Add the water and mix until it forms a dough. Wrap in clingfilm and put into the fridge to rest for 2 hours.

Preheat the oven to 160°C/fan 140°C/gas 3 and line a baking tray with baking paper.

Take the dough out of the fridge and let it soften for about 15 minutes, then roll it out on a lightly floured surface until it is 5mm thick. Using a 7cm cutter, cut out rounds and place them on the prepared baking tray. Bake for 15 minutes, until golden brown.

Leave for 4–5 minutes on the tray, then put them on a rack to cool.

Makes about 40

Suitable for freezing (uncooked dough or cooked biscuits)

Preparation time: 25 minutes

Proving/resting time: 2 hours

Cooking time: 15 minutes

440g plain wholemeal flour

15g baking powder (4 level teaspoons)

125g medium or coarse oatmeal

100g caster sugar

480g cold unsalted butter, diced small

50ml cold water

Left to right: rye crackers, poppy seed and black onion crisps, oat and wheat biscuits

POPPY SEED AND BLACK ONION CRISPS

Lovely with soft goat's cheese – just watch out, as they are very addictive. They keep for a couple of weeks in an airtight tin.

Whisk the oil and water together in a large jug or bowl. Put all the other ingredients into a large bowl, add the liquid and mix together. Once the mixture has formed into a dough, take it out of the bowl and knead on a lightly floured surface until it is smooth. Wrap in clingfilm and leave to rest overnight.

Preheat the oven to 200°C/fan 180°C/gas 6 and line two large baking trays with baking paper.

On a lightly floured surface, roll out the dough to about 3mm thick and cut out rounds using a 4cm round cutter. Then roll each round out again to 1mm thick. Brush off any excess flour and put them on the prepared baking trays. Bake for 8–10 minutes, until golden brown. Watch out – they burn really easily. Depending on the size of your trays you may need to do these in more than one batch.

Store in an airtight container.

Make about 50

Suitable for freezing (cooked or raw dough)

Preparation time: 30 minutes

Proving/resting time: overnight

Cooking time: 10 minutes

200ml rapeseed oil
290ml water
4 teaspoons black onion seeds
4 teaspoons poppy seeds
2 teaspoons fine sea salt
2 teaspoons caster sugar
600g plain flour
2 teaspoons baking powder

RYE CRACKERS

These have a wonderful crunch and a deep rye flavour. Great with any cheese, but also nice to use as canapés or as a starter with various toppings.

Put the rye flour, sugar and salt into a large bowl and mix together. Pour in the water and mix until it comes together into a ball, then wrap in clingfilm and put into the fridge for a few hours to rest.

Preheat the oven to 200°C/fan 180°C/gas 6 and line a baking tray with baking paper.

Cut the dough into four pieces. On a lightly floured surface, roll out each piece of dough as thinly as you can, about 16cm square and 2mm thick, and place on the prepared baking tray. Using a fork, prick the rolled-out dough all over and bake for 8–12 minutes, until crisp and golden brown.

Place on a rack to cool, then break into small pieces and serve.

Makes 4 large crackers
Suitable for freezing (uncooked dough or cooked crackers)
Preparation time: 15 minutes
Proving/resting time: 3 hours
Cooking time: 12 minutes

200g wholegrain rye flour
1 teaspoon caster sugar
½ teaspoon fine sea salt
120ml water

DOUGHNUTS

I started making my doughnuts while working at St John Restaurant over ten years ago, and if I say so myself they have become a bit legendary. Once you've had my doughnuts there is no going back.

I normally keep the fillings quite classic – custard, jam, lemon curd and apple cinnamon. But I have been developing many new flavours for this book, like my most fought-over one, the caramel custard with salted honeycomb sprinkle, which has become a bit of a signature for me, and another that I launched at Glastonbury, the violet custard with sugared violets and Parma violet sprinkle.

As in my bread recipes, I always weigh the water when I'm making doughnuts; it's a lot more accurate than using a measuring jug.

I would recommend using a deep-fat fryer (you can pick up a Breville 3 litre one for about £30), which is a lot safer than a pan of hot oil. Either way, PLEASE be careful when using hot oil – I have had many burns and it's really not very nice.

You will also need an electric mixer such as a Kenwood or KitchenAid, and if you don't have a deep-fat fryer (which will have an integral thermometer) you will need a good digital thermometer to check that the oil is at the right temperature.

You can try out your own fillings by using the recipe for crème patissière and just folding in your additional filling of choice, but I am not a fan of the savoury doughnuts that are popping up in a few places.

THE DOUGHNUT DOUGH

Put all the dough ingredients apart from the butter into the bowl of an electric mixer with a beater attachment and mix on a medium speed for 8 minutes, or until the dough starts coming away from the sides and forms a ball.

Turn off the mixer and let the dough rest for 1 minute. Take care that your mixer doesn't overheat – it needs to rest as well as the dough!

Start the mixer up again on a medium speed and slowly add the butter to the dough – about 25g at a time. Once it is all incorporated, mix on high speed for 5 minutes, until the dough is glossy, smooth and very elastic when pulled, then cover the bowl with clingfilm and leave to prove until it has doubled in size. Knock back the dough, then re-cover the bowl and put into the fridge to chill overnight.

The next day, take the dough out of the fridge and cut it into 50g pieces (you should get about 20). Roll them into smooth, taut, tight buns and place them on a floured baking tray, leaving plenty of room between them as you don't want them to stick together while they prove. Cover lightly with clingfilm and leave for about 4 hours, or until about doubled in size.

Get your deep-fat fryer ready, or get a heavy-based saucepan and fill it up to the halfway point with rapeseed oil (please be extremely careful, as hot oil is very dangerous). Heat the oil to 180°C.

When the oil is heated to the correct temperature, carefully remove the doughnuts from the tray by sliding a floured pastry scraper underneath them, taking care not to deflate them, and put them into the oil. Do not overcrowd the fryer – do 2–3 per batch, depending on the size of your pan. Fry for 2 minutes on each side until golden brown – they puff up and float, so you may need to gently push them down after about a minute to help them colour evenly. Remove from the fryer and place on kitchen paper, then toss them in a bowl of caster sugar while still warm. Repeat until all are fried, BUT make sure the oil temperature is correct every time before you fry – if it is too high they will colour too quickly and burn, and will be raw in the middle, and if it is too low the oil will be absorbed into the doughnut and it will become greasy. Set aside to cool before filling.

Makes about 20 doughnuts (about 1kg dough)
Preparation time: 45 minutes, plus proving and overnight chilling
Cooking time: 4 minutes per doughnut, fried in batches; about 30–40 minutes total

FOR THE DOUGH
500g strong white bread flour
60g caster sugar
10g fine sea salt
15g fresh yeast, crumbled
4 eggs
zest of ½ lemon
150g water
125g softened unsalted butter

FOR COOKING
about 2 litres sunflower oil, for deep-frying

FOR TOSSING
caster sugar

To fill the doughnuts, make a hole in the crease of each one (anywhere around the white line between the fried top and bottom). Fill a piping bag with your desired filling and pipe into the doughnut until swollen with pride. Roughly 20–50g is the optimum quantity, depending on the filling; cream will be less, because it is more aerated. You can fit in more than this, but it doesn't give such a good balance of dough to filling.

The doughnuts are best eaten straight away, but will keep in an airtight tin and can be reheated to refresh them.

CUSTARD
(CRÈME PATISSIÈRE)

Slit the vanilla pod open lengthways and scrape out the seeds. Put both pod and seeds into a heavy-based saucepan with the milk and bring slowly just to the boil, to infuse the vanilla.

Meanwhile place the egg yolks and the 125g of sugar in a bowl and mix together for a few seconds, then sift in the flour and mix again.

Pour the just-boiling milk over the yolk mixture, whisking constantly to prevent curdling, then return the mixture to the saucepan. Cook over a medium heat, whisking constantly for about 5 minutes, until very thick.

Pass through a fine sieve, discarding the vanilla, and place a sheet of clingfilm on the surface of the custard to prevent a skin forming. Leave to cool, then refrigerate.

Whip the cream and the 2 tablespoons of sugar together until thick but not over-whipped and fold into the chilled custard.

Makes about 900g (45g filling each for 20 doughnuts)
Preparation time: 20 minutes
Cooking time: 5 minutes

1 vanilla pod
500ml full fat milk
6 egg yolks
125g caster sugar, plus an extra 2 tablespoons
80g plain flour
200ml double cream

FILLINGS FOR THE DOUGHNUTS USING CUSTARD (CRÈME PATISSIÈRE)

PLAIN CUSTARD – see page 146 (45g each for 20 doughnuts).

SAFFRON – add a good pinch of saffron to the milk. Finish with half the quantity of cream. Will yield 100g less, i.e. about 800g (40g each for 20 doughnuts).

COFFEE – add 4 tablespoons of freshly ground strong coffee to the milk (45g each for 20 doughnuts).

CHOCOLATE – whisk 150g dark chocolate (70%) into the milk. Finish with half the cream. Will yield about 900g (45g each for 20 doughnuts).

MALT AND VANILLA – mix 2 tablespoons of powdered malt into the sugar, and 2 tablespoons of liquid malt into the milk. Will yield about 800g (40g each for 20 doughnuts).

BROWN SUGAR – replace the caster sugar with half soft dark brown sugar and half light brown sugar. You can also add some chopped stem ginger to the finished crème patissière, or some hazelnut praline. Finish with half the quantity of cream (makes 40g each for 20 doughnuts).

VIOLET CUSTARD – add 3 teaspoons of violet extract and 3 tablespoons of violet liqueur to the finished crème patissière, and sprinkle sugared violets and crushed Parma violet sweets over the top of the filled doughnuts (makes 45g each for 20 doughnuts).

CARAMEL CUSTARD AND SALTED HONEYCOMB SPRINKLE

The honeycomb sprinkle needs to be added just before serving, as it won't stay crunchy and it doesn't stick easily to the doughnuts.

Put the 250g of caster sugar into a heavy-based saucepan and let it dissolve slowly, then on a medium heat turn it into a dark brown caramel (don't go too far, or it will burn and become too bitter; it should take approximately 20–30 minutes). Once the right colour is reached, stop the caramel going any further by taking the pan off the heat and adding the milk (watch out, as it will spit and boil once the milk is added). Then return it to a low heat and melt the caramel into the milk.

Meanwhile put the egg yolks and brown sugars into a bowl and mix together for a few seconds, then sift in the flour and mix again.

Bring the milk just to the boil and pour over the yolk mixture, whisking constantly to prevent curdling, then return the mixture to the pan. Cook over a medium heat, whisking constantly for about 4–5 minutes, until very thick.

Pass through a fine sieve and place a sheet of clingfilm on the surface of the custard to prevent a skin forming. Leave to cool, then refrigerate.

Whip the cream and the 2 tablespoons of caster sugar together until thick but not over-whipped and fold into the chilled custard.

Bash up the honeycomb with a good pinch of Maldon sea salt, using the end of a rolling pin, and sprinkle on top of your filled doughnuts.

Makes about 1 litre (50g filling each for 20 doughnuts)
Preparation time: 45 minutes
Cooking time: 5 minutes

250g caster sugar, plus
   2 tablespoons
500ml full fat milk
8 egg yolks
30g soft light brown sugar
30g soft dark brown sugar
90g plain flour
200ml double cream
honeycomb (see page 246)
Maldon sea salt

SEVILLE ORANGE CUSTARD WITH GINGER SNAP SPRINKLE

The ginger snaps need to be sprinkled over just before serving, to retain the crunch.

Zest and juice the oranges, then split the vanilla pod open lengthways and scrape out the seeds. Put the zest, seeds and pod into a heavy-based saucepan with the milk and bring slowly to the boil, to infuse with the zest and the vanilla. Set the orange juice aside to add later.

Meanwhile place the egg yolks and the 125g of caster sugar in a bowl and mix together for a few seconds, then sift in the flour and mix again.

Pour the just-boiling milk over the yolk mixture, whisking constantly to prevent curdling, then return the mixture to the saucepan. Cook over a medium heat, whisking constantly for about 5 minutes, until very thick, then gradually whisk in the orange juice.

Pass through a fine sieve and place a sheet of clingfilm on the surface of the custard to prevent a skin from forming. Discard the orange zest and vanilla pod. Leave to cool, then refrigerate.

Whip the cream and the 2 tablespoons of caster sugar together until thick but not over-whipped and fold into the chilled custard.

Break up the ginger snaps and sprinkle on top of your filled doughnuts.

Makes about 900g (45g filling each for 20 doughnuts)
Preparation time: 20 minutes
Cooking time: 5 minutes

2 Seville oranges
1 vanilla pod
500ml full fat milk
6 egg yolks
125g caster sugar, plus
    2 tablespoons
80g plain flour
200ml double cream
ginger snaps (see page 136)

CREAM
(CRÈME CHANTILLY)

Split the vanilla pod open lengthways and scrape out the seeds, discarding the pod. Add the seeds to the cream and sugar and whisk together until smooth, silky and thick, taking care not to over-whisk.

Makes about 200g (only enough for 10 doughnuts on its own, but you can use it to fold other fillings into)
Preparation time: 5 minutes

1 vanilla pod
200ml double cream
2 tablespoons caster sugar

FILLINGS FOR THE DOUGHNUTS USING CREAM (CRÈME CHANTILLY)

BLACKCURRANT – put 500g of blackcurrants, 100g of caster sugar and 1 tablespoon of cassis into a pan. Heat to dissolve the sugar, then bring to the boil and simmer until soft. Chill, then fold through the cream. Makes about 550g of purée, which when stirred into the cream gives a final total of about 750g (35g of filling each for 20 doughnuts).

STRAWBERRY – finely chop 500g of ripe strawberries, add a good pinch of finely chopped fresh mint and fold through the cream. Gives a total of 700g, enough to fill 20–30 doughnuts.

PEACH AND RASPBERRY – take 3 ripe peaches and finely dice, then add 200g of raspberries and 25g of caster sugar and pulp together. Leave for a couple of hours, then fold through the cream. Makes a total of 500g of filling (about 35g each for 15 doughnuts).

»

GOOSEBERRY AND ELDERFLOWER – put 500g of gooseberries, 120g of caster sugar and a splash of elderflower cordial into a pan. Heat to dissolve the sugar, then bring to the boil and simmer until soft. Once simmering, add a homemade teabag of fresh elderflowers (about 4 heads of flowers) and steep in the gooseberries until cool. Take out the elderflower teabag and sieve the gooseberries, then fold through the cream. Makes about 550g of purée, which when stirred into the cream gives a final total of approximately 750g (35g of filling for 20 doughnuts).

PASSION FRUIT – take 5 passion fruits, scoop out the pulp and whiz in a food processor until blitzed. Pour into a saucepan with 50g of caster sugar and put on a low heat to dissolve the sugar, then strain, chill, and whisk through the cream. Makes a total of about 300g (35g each for 10 doughnuts).

BLOOD ORANGE CURD – see page 244. Fold the curd through the cream until the taste is to your liking. Use about 40–45g of filling in each doughnut.

LEMON CURD – see page 244. Fold the curd through the cream until the taste is to your liking. Use about 40–45g of filling in each doughnut.

PINEAPPLE AND RUM – put 500g of pineapple (peeled, cored and diced small) and 50g of sugar into a pan. Heat to dissolve the sugar, then bring to the boil and simmer until soft. Add a good splash of rum and leave to cool, then strain and fold through the cream. This gives about 700g final weight of filling (35g of filling each for 20 doughnuts).

OTHER FILLINGS

(should each fill about 20 doughnuts)

JAM – fill the doughnuts with about 30g of jam (see page 241).

BLACKBERRY AND APPLE – put 600g of peeled and cored apples into a pan with 100g of caster sugar. Heat to dissolve the sugar, then bring to the boil and simmer gently for about 20 minutes. While still hot stir in 450g of blackberries, mush together and chill. This gives about 1kg of purée, enough to fill 20 doughnuts with a generous 50g filling.

APPLE AND CINNAMON – put 800g of peeled and cored apples into a pan with 150g of light brown sugar and ½ a stick of cinnamon. Heat to dissolve the sugar, then bring to the boil and simmer gently for about 20 minutes. Take out the cinnamon stick and discard, then cool and chill. Add a pinch of ground cinnamon to the tossing sugar. This makes about 800g, enough to fill 20 doughnuts with 40g of filling.

APRICOT AND CAMOMILE – put 600g of stoned apricots into a pan with 150g of caster sugar. Heat to dissolve the sugar, then bring to the boil and simmer lightly until soft. Add a couple of camomile teabags and leave to cool. Once cool, take out the teabags and strain, then whiz the apricots in a food processor. Makes 750g, enough to fill 20 doughnuts.

DEEP-FRIED JAM SANDWICH

If you don't have time to make doughnuts, this is a very good substitute. A brioche loaf may also work well here.

First make the batter. Whisk the eggs and milk together, then sift the flour and salt into a large bowl. Slowly whisk the egg and milk mixture into the flour, then pass through a fine sieve into a shallow bowl large enough to take a whole slice of bread.

Get your deep-fat fryer ready, or get a heavy-based saucepan and fill it halfway up with sunflower oil (please be very careful, as hot oil is very dangerous). Heat the oil to 180°C.

Butter the bread and spread 4 of the slices with the jam. Sandwich together firmly, trying not to let the jam ooze out.

When the oil is heated to the correct temperature, dip the sandwich in the batter mix until it is all covered evenly. Fry in the hot oil for 2 minutes on each side, until golden brown and crispy. Remove with a slotted spatula and drain on kitchen paper.

Repeat until all 4 sandwiches are fried, but make sure the oil temperature is correct each time, as if it is too high they will colour too quickly and burn and the middle will not feel the heat, and if it is too low the oil will be absorbed into the batter and it will become greasy.

Toss in caster sugar, sprinkled on a plate. Serve whole or cut into slices, with a large dollop of whipped cream or on their own.

Makes 4 sandwiches
Preparation time: 10 minutes
Cooking time: 4 minutes per
    sandwich (16 minutes total)

sunflower oil, for deep-frying
8 slices of white bread
jam of your choice
    (see page 241)
butter
caster sugar, for tossing

FOR THE BATTER
4 eggs
100ml milk
80g plain flour
a pinch of fine sea salt

WARM TO HOT PUDDINGS

Warm to hot puddings are the most comforting kind, the sort of puddings you would have after Sunday lunch, bringing back childhood memories and even thoughts of school dinners. However, over the years a lot of these puddings have been bastardized and have become too sweet and heavy – and some of the names have even been changed, for example spotted dick becoming spotted Richard...

In this chapter you will find a few classics such as spotted dick, bread pudding, tapioca and apple pie, all of which I have served in Michelin-starred restaurants, so please don't think of these sorts of puddings as anything other than beautifully delicious. (I have even had a poem written about my marmalade sponge...)

You will need to make sure you have a good few ovenproof pudding basins (Mason Cash make the best ones), as well as a good deep roasting tray and lots of mixing bowls.

Suet adds a lovely richness to puddings and pastry. It's the fat that surrounds beef and sheep kidneys, and you can ask for it at your butcher's, but if you do you will need to devein it first, then mince it. Otherwise use a packet of Atora suet instead, which is available at most supermarkets and is very good.

STEAMED MARMALADE SPONGE AND WHISKY CUSTARD

Good for those winter months, this is a really moist, light, rich and warming sponge, with the thick-cut bitter marmalade off-setting the sweet sponge beautifully. I have served it for many Burns' Night dinners and have even had a poem written about it. The whisky custard works very happily with many other puddings, like ginger and clementine pudding (page 167) and apple pie (page 172).

Serves 4–6

Not suitable for freezing

Preparation time: pudding 20 minutes, custard 5 minutes

Cooking time: pudding 2½ hours, custard 15 minutes

Preheat the oven to 160°C/fan 140°C/gas 3 and grease and flour a 1 litre pudding basin.

In an electric mixer with a beater attachment, or in a bowl with a wooden spoon, cream your butter and sugars together until light and fluffy. Gradually add the eggs one at a time, mixing as you go to prevent them curdling, then mix in the sifted flour and baking powder.

Fold in the milk and 2 tablespoons of the marmalade.

Put the remaining 4 tablespoons of marmalade into the bottom of the prepared basin and spoon the sponge mix on top. Cover the top with a buttered round of baking paper, then cover that with a piece of foil with a pleat in the middle and tie with string to secure.

Place the pudding in a deep roasting tray and pour boiling water into the tray to come halfway up the sides of the basin. Cover the whole thing with foil and bake for 2½ hours.

Remove the pudding carefully from the baking tray and leave for 10 minutes before unwrapping, unmoulding and upturning on a serving plate.

While the pudding is resting, make the whisky custard. Slit the vanilla pod open lengthways and scrape out the seeds. Put the seeds and pod into a heavy-based saucepan with the milk and cream and bring slowly to the boil to infuse the vanilla.

Meanwhile put the egg yolks and sugar into a bowl and mix together for a few seconds.

Pour the boiling milk into the yolks, whisking constantly to prevent curdling, then return the mixture to the saucepan. Cook slowly over a low heat, stirring constantly with a wooden spoon, until it thickens enough to coat the back of the spoon.

Pour through a fine sieve, discard the vanilla pod, and stir in the whisky. Serve straight away, in a jug, with the pudding.

160g softened unsalted butter, plus extra for greasing

100g caster sugar

50g soft light brown sugar

2 eggs

230g plain flour, sifted, plus extra for dusting

1½ teaspoons baking powder

4 tablespoons whole milk

6 tablespoons marmalade (see page 243)

FOR THE WHISKY CUSTARD

1 vanilla pod

250ml full fat milk

125ml double cream

3 egg yolks

80g caster sugar

30–40ml good whisky

RUM BABA

These sponges are beautifully soft and pillowy, and once soaked in syrup and served with lashings of cold whipped cream, wow! – what a joy.

Put the yeast and eggs into the bowl of an electric mixer and whisk together. Add the flour, sugar, orange zest and salt, then, using a beater attachment, mix together for 5 minutes. Cover with clingfilm and leave for 1 hour somewhere warm, until doubled in size.

Meanwhile, grease and flour 6 rum baba moulds or individual dariole moulds and pop a circle of baking paper at the bottom of each one. Place them on a baking tray.

Put the bowl of dough back on the mixer and gradually add the softened butter. Mix until the dough is elastic – about 5 minutes – then add the raisins.

Place the mixture on a lightly floured surface and bring together, adding a little more flour if necessary to make it manageable. Divide the dough into 6 pieces and put them into the moulds – they should be three-quarters full. Cover lightly with clingfilm and place somewhere warm for about 1–1½ hours, or until risen to the top of the moulds.

Preheat the oven to 200°C/fan 180°C/gas 4 and bake the babas for 12–15 minutes, or until firm and golden brown. Take them out of the oven and unmould them, then place them on a rack to cool for 10 minutes.

While the babas are in the oven, make the syrup. Put all the ingredients into a large saucepan and bring to the boil, then take out the strips of lemon and orange rind and the cinnamon stick. Put back on the heat and simmer until you have a shiny, slightly thickened syrup (it will take about 15 minutes of vigorous simmering).

Put the still warm babas into a dish and pour the hot syrup over them, gently turning them so that they are all covered. Leave for 15 minutes, turning occasionally, until soaked through.

Serve warm, with rum-soaked raisins and lashings of cold whipped cream.

Serves 6
Suitable for freezing (minus the syrup)
Preparation time: 30 minutes
Proving time: 2½ hours
Cooking time: 40 minutes

10g fresh yeast, crumbled
4 eggs
250g strong plain bread flour, plus extra for dusting
10g caster sugar
zest of ½ an orange
a pinch of fine sea salt
125g unsalted butter, softened, plus extra for greasing
40g rum-soaked raisins, drained (see page 240), plus extra for serving
200ml whipped double cream, to serve

FOR THE SYRUP
400ml water
300g caster sugar
180ml dark rum
¼ of a stick of cinnamon
3 strips of lemon rind
3 strips of orange rind

BREAD PUDDING AND BUTTERSCOTCH SAUCE

This is the perfect way to use leftover stale bread; you can serve it up as a great dessert, as I have done in the past in many restaurants, and it's also lovely on picnics or when you're on the go, as it holds together very well once cooled.

Remove the crusts from the bread, then roughly tear it up and put it into a large bowl. Cover with water and leave to stand for about 30 minutes.

Preheat the oven to 180°C/fan 160°C/gas 4 and grease a 2 litre ovenproof dish.

Put the rest of the pudding ingredients, except the demerara sugar, into a large bowl and mix together until all is incorporated.

Squeeze all the excess water out of the bread, then add to the bowl of pudding ingredients and mix together well. Pop the mix into the prepared dish and place on a baking tray. Sprinkle the top of the pudding with the demerara sugar and bake for 1 hour, until crisp and golden brown on top.

To make the sauce, put the caster sugar and water into a heavy-based saucepan and place over a gentle heat. Once the sugar is melted, turn the heat up slightly and let it turn to a caramel – you want it fairly dark. When it has reached that point, take it off the heat and add the cream (watch out, as it will spit a bit and boil furiously), whisking to combine. Put back on a low heat to dissolve the caramel into the cream, which will take a minute or so. Take off the heat and whisk in the butter, then strain through a sieve.

Serve the bread pudding with the hot butterscotch sauce and vanilla ice cream.

Serves 6–8

Not suitable for freezing

Preparation time: pudding 15 minutes, sauce 5 minutes

Cooking time: pudding 1 hour, sauce 10 minutes

FOR THE PUDDING

400g stale white bread, sliced

softened butter, for greasing

65g shredded suet

120g soft dark brown sugar

70g raisins

30g sultanas

1 small Bramley apple, peeled, cored and thinly sliced

1 egg, beaten

1 teaspoon mixed spice

¼ teaspoon ground allspice

a pinch of ground cinnamon

2 tablespoons dark rum

zest of ½ an orange

2 tablespoons demerara sugar

FOR THE BUTTERSCOTCH SAUCE

250g caster sugar

2 tablespoons water

500ml double cream

125g softened unsalted butter

PEACH AND AMARETTO COBBLER

I always think of cobbled streets when I pull this out of the oven. You can use lots of different fruits for this recipe, but I love peaches and rosemary because they go so well with the almond cobbles.

First make the cobbler dough. Dice the butter into small chunks and put them into a bowl with the flour, sugar, salt and orange zest. Rub together with your fingertips until the mixture is like fine crumbs, then add the beaten egg, milk and almond essence and mix until a dough is formed. Wrap it in clingfilm and put it into the fridge for about 2–3 hours, to firm up.

While the dough is resting, make the filling. Halve the peaches and discard the stones, then cut them into quarters. Melt the butter in a saucepan and add the quartered peaches, rosemary and sugar, then cook over a low heat until just starting to collapse, shaking the pan occasionally. Take off the heat and stir in the amaretto, then transfer to a 2–3 litre ovenproof dish, cool slightly and remove the rosemary sprigs.

Preheat the oven to 180°C/fan 160°C/gas 4.

Take the dough out of the fridge and let it soften slightly, then roll it out on a lightly floured working surface to a thickness of 1.5cm. Using a 4cm cutter, cut out 12 rounds, re-rolling until all the pastry is used up. Place the rounds of dough over the cooked peaches until more or less covered, then eggwash the top, scatter a few flaked almonds on top of some of the cobbles, and sprinkle with the tablespoon of caster sugar.

Bake for about 25–30 minutes, until the cobbles are golden brown and baked through.

Serve with double cream or custard.

Serves 6

Not suitable for freezing

Preparation time: 25 minutes, plus chilling time

Cooking time: 30 minutes

FOR THE FILLING

5 ripe peaches

20g unsalted butter

2 sprigs of rosemary

20g demerara sugar

30ml amaretto liqueur

FOR THE COBBLER TOPPING

50g unsalted butter

225g self-raising flour, plus extra for dusting

110g caster sugar, plus 1 tablespoon for sprinkling

a pinch of fine sea salt

zest of ½ an orange

1 egg, beaten

2 tablespoons milk

1 teaspoon almond essence

1 egg, beaten, to glaze

2 tablespoons flaked almonds

PRUNE, ARMAGNAC AND ALMOND PUDDING

This is a lovely light pudding which really showcases the Armagnac prunes to perfection and is fairly easy to put together.

Preheat the oven to 160°C/fan 140°C/gas 3 and thoroughly grease a 2–3 litre ovenproof dish.

Put the honey and butter into a small saucepan and melt them together on a low heat, then take off the heat and leave to cool a little.

Put the eggs, yolks and sugar into the bowl of an electric mixer with a whisk attachment and whiz for about 5 minutes on a high speed. Fold in the melted butter and honey and the Armagnac syrup, and once incorporated add the ground almonds, vanilla extract and milk and fold in again.

Place your soaked prunes in the prepared dish, making sure they are scattered evenly.

Pour the pudding mixture over the prunes and bake for 40–45 minutes, or until golden brown and cooked through.

Serve hot, with a large jug of cold double cream or custard.

Serves 4–6
Not suitable for freezing
Preparation time: 20 minutes
Cooking time: 45 minutes

150g butter, plus lots of soft
   butter for greasing
50g runny honey
2 eggs
2 egg yolks
150g caster sugar
1 tablespoon Armagnac syrup
   from the soaked prunes
150g ground almonds
1 tablespoon vanilla extract
2 tablespoons full fat milk
300g prunes in Armagnac
   (see page 240), drained

STICKY BANANA PUDDING

The full credit for this recipe goes to my mother-in-law, Pamela Reynolds, who has made this pudding for me countless times for Sunday lunch. I have served it in many restaurants in London.

Serves 4–6
Not suitable for freezing
Preparation time: 20 minutes
Cooking time: 2 hours

Preheat the oven to 160°C/ fan 140°C/gas 3 and grease and flour a 1 litre pudding basin.

In an electric mixer with a beater attachment, or in a bowl with a wooden spoon, cream your butter and sugar together until light and fluffy. Gradually add the eggs, one at a time, mixing as you go to prevent them curdling, then mix in the sifted flour and Camp coffee.

Peel the bananas and chop them into 2cm pieces, then fold them into the sponge mixture. Spoon it into the prepared pudding basin. Place a circle of baking paper on top, cover that with a piece of foil with a pleat in the middle, and tie with a piece of string to secure.

Place the pudding in a deep roasting tray and pour in boiling water to come halfway up the sides of the basin. Cover the whole thing with foil and bake for 2 hours.

Serve hot, with hot butterscotch sauce (see page 161) and vanilla ice cream.

85g softened unsalted butter, plus extra for greasing
175g self-raising flour, sifted, plus extra for dusting
140g caster sugar
2 eggs
2½ teaspoons Camp chicory and coffee essence
2 or 3 small bananas

POOR KNIGHTS OF WINDSOR

This French toast/eggy bread style dessert is named after the Poor Knights of Windsor – an order of military pensioners founded in 1349.

Put the milk, sugar, Madeira, egg and yolk into a large bowl and whisk together. Lay the bread in a large flat tray (one with sides), then pour over the mix and leave to soak for 30 minutes.

Melt half the butter and oil in a large non-stick frying pan. Once it is hot, put 4 soaked slices into the pan and fry on a medium heat for about 4 minutes on each side, or until golden brown and starting to caramelize. Keep them warm in a low oven while you finish the other slices, repeating until all the bread is finished.

Serve warm, cut into triangles, with crème fraîche or whipped cream, and drizzle over some honey or maple syrup.

Serves 4
Not suitable for freezing
Preparation time: 5 minutes, plus
    30 minutes soaking time
Cooking time: 20 minutes

285ml full fat milk
50g caster sugar
60ml Madeira
1 egg
1 egg yolk
8 slices of stale white bread,
    crusts cut off
50g butter
2 tablespoons sunflower or
    rapeseed oil
honey or maple syrup,
    for drizzling

GINGER AND CLEMENTINE PUDDING

This pudding is a great alternative to Christmas pudding and a good way of using a few of those clementines at the bottom of your stocking. You can use 2 oranges, if clementines are not around.

Preheat the oven to 160°C/fan 140°C/gas 3 and line a 20cm round springform cake tin, 7cm deep, with baking paper.

Zest, peel and segment the clementines and put them into a bowl. Chop the stem ginger into small dice and add to the bowl, then place the clementines and ginger in the bottom of your prepared cake tin.

Sift the flour, bicarbonate of soda, ground ginger, cinnamon and salt into a large bowl, then stir in the light brown sugar.

Put the water, golden syrup, black treacle and butter into a saucepan and melt together over a low heat. Pour on to the flour mix and whisk together, then add the egg and whisk in.

Pour the mixture into the cake tin on top of the clementines and bake for 45 minutes, until firm to the touch and a skewer comes out clean.

Turn out on to a rack to cool.

Serve while still warm, with crème fraîche.

Serves 4

Not suitable for freezing

Preparation time: 5 minutes, plus
  30 minutes soaking time

Cooking time: 45 minutes

4 clementines

2 chunks of stem ginger in
  syrup, drained

200g plain flour

1 teaspoon bicarbonate of soda

2 teaspoons ground ginger

½ teaspoon ground cinnamon

a pinch of fine sea salt

125g soft light brown sugar

150ml water

75g golden syrup

15g black treacle

100g unsalted butter

1 egg, beaten

SPOTTED DICK

This is one of the classics, served with lashings of custard, which can of course also be served with apple pie, mince pies, bread pudding and much, much more.

Preheat the oven to 160°C/fan 140°C/gas 3. Grease a 1 litre pudding basin with butter and dust with a little flour.

Sift the flour and baking powder into a large bowl, then mix in the suet and caster sugar. Add the lemon zest and currants and mix together. Now add the milk – stir in 125ml to start with, then use some or all of the rest of the milk if necessary. You are looking for a dropping consistency. Put to one side.

Pour the golden syrup into the bottom of your prepared pudding basin and place the butter on top of the syrup. Spoon your dick mixture on top of the syrup and butter. Place a round of baking paper on top, cover with a piece of foil (with a generous pleat in the middle) and secure with string.

Put the basin into a deep roasting tin and pour in enough boiling water to come halfway up the sides of the basin. Bake for about 2 hours, until well risen and firm to the touch (remembering to keep the water topped up).

Meanwhile, make the custard. Slit the vanilla pod open lengthways and scrape out the seeds. Put both seeds and pod into a heavy-based saucepan with the milk and cream and bring slowly to the boil, to infuse the vanilla.

Put the egg yolks and sugar into a bowl and mix together for a few seconds. Pour the boiling milk into the yolks, whisking constantly to prevent curdling, then return the mixture to the saucepan. Cook slowly over a low heat, stirring constantly with a wooden spoon, until it thickens enough to coat the back of the spoon.

Pour through a fine sieve and discard the vanilla pod, then pour the custard into a jug.

Turn out the spotted dick into a large bowl and serve hot, with the custard.

Serves 4
Not suitable for freezing
Preparation time: pudding 20 minutes, custard 5 minutes
Cooking time: pudding 2 hours, custard 15 minutes

10g softened butter, plus extra for greasing
250g plain flour, plus extra for dusting
8g baking powder
125g shredded suet
70g caster sugar
zest of 1 lemon
125g currants
125–250ml full fat milk
60g golden syrup

FOR THE CUSTARD
1 vanilla pod
250ml full fat milk
125ml double cream
3 egg yolks
80g caster sugar

MINCE PIES

You can start the mincemeat a good six months in advance, as it will keep happily and improves a little with age. I only make these at Christmas, as they're such a treat, served just warm, with cold extra thick cream.

First make the mincemeat. Peel and core the cooking apples and chop them into small dice, then put them into a very large bowl, big enough to fit all the ingredients in. Add to the bowl all the ingredients apart from the brandy and rum and mix together. Cover, then leave overnight in a cool place (not in the fridge).

Preheat the oven to 120°C/ fan 100°C/gas ½.

Place all the mincemeat mix in a large deep roasting tray. Cover with foil and put into the oven for about 1 hour, stirring every 20 minutes. Once baked, take out of the oven and cool for about 30 minutes. Stir in the brandy and rum and place in sterilized jars.

Next make the pie crust. Put the flour, butter and caster sugar into the bowl of an electric mixer with a beater attachment and mix until it just comes together. Whisk the egg and yolk together and slowly mix in – adding only enough for the mixture to start coming together – for about 30 seconds. Bring the dough together with your hands, then wrap in clingfilm and place in the fridge for 3–4 hours or overnight.

Butter and flour a 12-hole deep muffin tray. Take the pastry out of the fridge and let it soften for about 1½ hours, then roll it out on a floured surface to 5–6mm thick. Using a 10cm cutter, cut out 12 circles for the base of the pies, re-rolling when necessary. Re-roll the pastry again, then, using a 7cm cutter, cut out 12 circles for the tops.

Line the holes in the muffin tray with the larger circles of pastry, letting them overhang. Spoon about 3 heaped tablespoons of mincemeat into each one and cover with the smaller circles. Eggwash the pies, then bring up the overhanging pastry round the sides and seal on to the top. Sprinkle with demerara sugar. Cut a small slit in the top to act as a steam-hole and leave to rest in the fridge for 2 hours.

Preheat the oven to 160°C/fan 140°C/gas 3 and bake the pies for about 40 minutes, until golden brown. Leave in the tin for 5 minutes, then take them out carefully, releasing them all the way round first with a small palette or cutlery knife. Place on a rack to cool – best served warm straight away, or cooled and re-warmed later. They store well for 2–3 days in an airtight tin. Serve with extra thick Jersey cream.

Makes 12

Not suitable for freezing

Preparation time: 25 minutes for mincemeat, 25 minutes for pie preparation; plus chilling/ resting time

Cooking time: 1 hour for mincemeat, 40 minutes for pies

FOR THE MINCEMEAT

500g cooking apples

500g suet

500g sultanas

500g currants

500g raisins

500g soft dark brown sugar

zest and juice of 4 lemons

zest and juice of 4 oranges

125g nibbed or flaked almonds

3 tablespoons ground mixed spice

2 teaspoons ground cinnamon

2 teaspoons grated nutmeg

250ml brandy

50ml dark rum

FOR THE PIE CRUST

375g strong plain bread flour, plus extra for dusting

225g cold unsalted butter, cubed, plus extra for greasing

150g caster sugar

1 whole egg

1 egg yolk

1 egg, beaten, to glaze

2 tablespoons demerara sugar

CHRISTMAS PUDDING

This recipe was handed down to me by my mum, Sally Ann Gellatly, and it was passed down to her by her mother. We always make it over a year in advance, to deepen the flavour, and feed it a few times with brandy.

First, put all the dry ingredients into a very large bowl (it will need to fit all the ingredients in) and mix together.

Now mix all the liquid ingredients together. Pour the liquid ingredients into the dry ingredients and mix very well – don't forget to give everyone a turn to stir and make a wish, and don't forget to pop your 50p piece in. Leave overnight in the fridge.

Preheat the oven to 160°C/fan 140°C/gas 3. Fill a 1 litre pudding basin with the mixture and cover the top with a round of baking paper. Cover that with a piece of foil, and tie with a piece of string. Place the pudding in a deep roasting tray and pour in boiling water to come halfway up the sides of the basin. Cover the whole thing with foil and place in the oven for 4 hours.

Leave until cool, then take off the baking paper and foil, clean up the basin and wrap it in clingfilm. Leave it until Christmas. If you are making this early in the year, you can feed it a few times with a bit more brandy. Just unwrap the pudding and stab a few holes in the top – drizzle over a couple of tablespoons every 3 months.

On Christmas Day, take off the clingfilm and rewrap with baking paper and foil. Depending on the size of your oven, you can either reheat it in the oven or on top of the stove in a steamer – it will take about 2 hours to reheat.

Remove the pudding from the bowl and place on a plate. Pour brandy over and light with a match.

Serve with a jug of cold cream. If you have any leftovers, chill, slice and fry with bacon for breakfast. Hey, it is Christmas.

Serves 10–12
Not suitable for freezing
Preparation time: 1 hour
Cooking time: 4 hours, plus
    reheating time

125g raisins
100g sultanas
200g currants
125g pitted prunes, chopped
75g peeled, cored and diced
    cooking apples
60g fresh white breadcrumbs
50g self-raising flour
125g soft dark brown sugar
25g mixed peel, finely chopped
10g nibbed or flaked almonds
15g whole almonds, roughly chopped
15g walnuts, roughly chopped
75g shredded suet
1 teaspoon ground mixed spice
1 teaspoon ground nutmeg
a pinch of ground allspice
a pinch of ground ginger
a pinch of ground cinnamon
a small pinch of ground cloves
zest and juice of ½ an orange
zest and juice of ½ a lemon
15g black treacle
2 eggs
75ml stout
30ml brandy, plus some to feed
    if ageing the pud
25ml tawny port
25ml dark rum
a 50p piece (optional – sterilize by
    soaking in sterilizing fluid overnight
    or boiling for 15 minutes)

APPLE PIE

This apple pie has a lovely crisp pastry top and bottom. I use a layer of sponge to soak up all those juices, to avoid a soggy bottom. And I don't use any spices, as I like the apple to sing out.

To make the pie crust, put the flour, salt, butter and sugar into the bowl of an electric mixer with a beater attachment and mix until it just comes together. Slowly add the egg and yolk and mix for about 1 minute, until incorporated. Bring together on a lightly floured surface (it is quite sticky at this point), then wrap in clingfilm and chill in the fridge for 3–4 hours or overnight.

Take the pastry out of the fridge and cut off a third. Put to one side with the other two-thirds of the pastry and let them soften for about 1½ hours. Meanwhile, grease and flour a 30cm loose-bottomed tart tin, 3–4cm deep.

On a floured surface, roll out the bigger piece of pastry into a circle 3mm thick and large enough to fill the tart case, leaving 1cm overhanging. Line the tart case with the pastry and put into the fridge to chill for 1 hour.

Peel and core the apples, then slice them thinly and put them into a large bowl. Stir in the sugar and put to one side.

Take the tart case out of the fridge and cover the base of the pastry with the sponge, cut into slices 5mm thick. Pour in the apple mix.

Using the third of pastry you have left, plus any trimmings from the base, roll out on a floured surface into a 3mm thick circle and place over the apples. Seal the top and bottom together, trimming off any excess. With any trimmings of pastry you have left over, make some leaves for decoration, using eggwash to stick them on.

Place in the fridge for 1 more hour.

Preheat the oven to 180°C/fan 160°C/gas 4 and glaze the whole pie with eggwash. Cut a little steam-hole in the top of the pastry with a small sharp knife. Place the pie on a baking tray (in case some of the juices escape), and bake for about 50 minutes, until golden brown.

Cool slightly on a rack, then take off the tart tin and serve on a large plate, with vanilla ice cream or custard.

You can add more fillings if you like, for example a handful of blackberries or raspberries.

Serves 8–10
Not suitable for freezing
Preparation time: 45 minutes, plus chilling time
Cooking time: 50 minutes

FOR THE APPLE FILLING
3 small Bramley apples
4 Braeburn apples
100g demerara sugar
150g sponge (see page 207 – freeze the rest for trifles or more pies)

FOR THE PIE CRUST
375g strong plain bread flour, plus extra for dusting
a pinch of fine sea salt
225g cold unsalted butter, plus extra for greasing
150g caster sugar
1 whole egg
1 egg yolk
1 egg, beaten, to glaze

STEAMED APPLE AND RHUBARB SUET PUDDING

Rhubarb is one of my favourite fruits (although I know it's classed as a vegetable) and I grow a lot of it in the garden. When paired with apple it's a match made in heaven. The suet pastry adds a deep richness to the dish.

Put all the pastry ingredients apart from the milk into a mixing bowl and rub together for a few minutes. Add the milk and mix together until a firm dough is formed, then wrap in clingfilm and put into the fridge for a few hours.

Preheat the oven to 160°C/fan 140°C/gas 3. Grease and flour a 1 litre pudding basin and place a small circle of baking paper in the bottom.

Put the sliced apples into a saucepan with the caster sugar and cook on a medium heat until the apple is soft. Leave to cool, then stir in the sliced rhubarb, orange juice, brown sugar, ground ginger and cornflour. Leave to one side.

On a lightly floured work surface, roll out the suet pastry into a circle 30cm in diameter and 3–4mm thick. Line the inside of the pudding basin with it – a lot will overhang, but it's easier to use a bigger round of pastry and then trim it. Push it into the corners, then trim the pastry with a clean pair of kitchen scissors, leaving 1cm all the way round. Roll out the leftover pastry on a lightly floured surface to make an even 15cm circle for the lid.

Fill the basin with your apple and rhubarb mix, then cover with the lid and brush with milk. Bring the overhanging pastry up over the lid and seal by crimping it. Place a greased circle of baking paper on top, then cover that with a piece of foil with a pleat in the middle and tie with a piece of string to secure.

Place the pudding in a deep roasting tray and pour in boiling water to come halfway up the sides of the basin. Cover the whole thing with more foil and bake for 2 hours, then take off the foil and the paper and put the pudding back into the oven naked for 10 more minutes, or until golden brown on top.

To serve, turn out the pudding into a large bowl and serve with a large jug of hot custard.

Serves 6
Not suitable for freezing
Preparation time: 30 minutes, plus chilling time
Cooking time: 2 hours 10 minutes

FOR THE SUET PASTRY

200g self-raising flour, plus extra for dusting
100g shredded suet
zest of ½ an orange
a pinch of fine sea salt
140ml milk, plus extra for brushing

FOR THE FILLING

2 Bramley apples, peeled, cored and cut into 0.5cm slices
60g caster sugar
250g rhubarb, trimmed and cut into 0.5cm slices
juice of 1 orange
40g soft light brown sugar
a pinch of ground ginger
2 tablespoons cornflour

CARDAMOM AND RUM BANANAS

You really need to make this dessert to order, so have everything measured out before you start. The cardamom and orange bring out the flavour of the bananas really well.

Deseed the cardamoms and crush the seeds to a powder in a pestle and mortar.

Put the sugar, butter, orange rind and juice and crushed cardamom seeds into a large, heavy-based non-stick frying pan on a low heat and melt together. Once melted, turn up the heat and cook for 3 minutes until you have a light brown caramel, stirring frequently so that the caramel is evenly distributed.

Add the peeled bananas (whole) and the rum, then flambé by tipping the pan into the gas flame – if cooking on an electric or induction hob use a match. While it's alight, keep the pan off the heat, then after about 30–40 seconds, once the flames have gone out, put back on a low heat. Cook the bananas at a light simmer for 3 minutes on each side, until they are soft and the sauce has reduced a little.

Serve straight away, with a generous scoop of vanilla ice cream.

Serves 4
Not suitable for freezing
Preparation time: 10 minutes
Cooking time: 10 minutes

12 whole green cardamoms
110g granulated sugar
45g unsalted butter, cubed
1 strip of orange rind
juice of 1 orange
4 bananas
200ml dark rum

BAY LEAF AND HONEY RICE PUDDING

This pudding has a lovely fragrance of bay and it's not overly sweet, as I only use honey (no sugar) in the recipe. And of course it has a great skin after it's baked.

Preheat the oven to 160°C/fan 140°C/gas 3.

Put the rice, honey, milk and bay leaves into a heavy-based casserole or a large oven dish and bring to the boil on a medium heat, stirring frequently. Bake uncovered for about 1 hour, until the top has a nice golden brown skin and the rice is cooked.

Leave to rest for 15 minutes before serving (this allows the excess liquid to be absorbed and the pudding to get creamy). Discard the bay leaves as you serve.

Serve hot, with a little jam, or just on its own.

Serves 4
Not suitable for freezing
Preparation time: 5 minutes
Cooking time: 1 hour, plus
    resting time

120g pudding rice
4 tablespoons runny honey
1 litre full fat milk
4 bay leaves
4 tablespoons jam, to serve
    (optional) (see page 241)

TAPIOCA

It's been voted the most hated school dinner a few times, but with this recipe I have changed quite a lot of minds. You can buy pearl tapioca in most supermarkets.

Put the tapioca and milk into a bowl and leave overnight in the fridge, to soak.

Slit the vanilla pod in half lengthways and scrape out the seeds. Put the seeds and pod into a medium, heavy-based saucepan with the milk and tapioca, then add the sugars and salt. Whisk in the beaten egg yolks, then bring slowly to a gentle simmer on a medium heat.

Cook until thick and creamy (about 8–9 minutes, stirring constantly so that it doesn't burn or stick). The tapioca is cooked through when it swells up and becomes almost translucent. Remove from the heat and allow to stand for 2 minutes before serving.

Serve warm, with a good dollop of jam and extra thick cream.

Makes 4 larger portions or
   6 smaller ones
Not suitable for freezing
Preparation time: 10 minutes,
   plus overnight soaking
Cooking time: 15 minutes

130g small pearl tapioca
750ml full fat milk
1 vanilla pod
75g caster sugar
a pinch of soft light brown sugar
a pinch of fine sea salt
2 egg yolks, beaten
jam (see page 241) and extra
   thick cream, to serve

TREACLE AND WALNUT TART

You can always make room for a slice of treacle tart. This keeps well for 3–4 days, so it's good for making in advance.

First make the pastry. In an electric mixer with a beater attachment, cream the butter and sugars together until white and fluffy, then add the egg yolks, one at a time to help prevent curdling. Sift the flour and salt and add to the mix, then combine until all is incorporated. Wrap in clingfilm and chill in the fridge for 5–6 hours.

Grease and flour a 25cm loose-bottomed tart case. Take the pastry out of the fridge and allow it to soften a little, so that you can roll it easily. Roll out the pastry on a lightly floured surface to about 3mm thick, and use it to line your prepared tart case. Put it into the fridge or freezer to chill for 2–3 hours.

Preheat the oven to 160°C/fan 140°C/Gas 3.

Take the tart case straight from the fridge or freezer, cover the pastry with clingfilm and fill with baking beans. Place on a baking sheet and bake for 15 minutes, or until the edges are golden brown, then remove the clingfilm and beans and put the tart case back into the oven for a further 15 minutes, or until it is golden brown all over (do not under-bake the tart case or you will have a soggy bottom). Remove from the oven and place on a rack to cool.

Increase the oven temperature to 180°C/fan 160°C/gas 4.

To make the filling, put the golden syrup, orange zest, juice, vanilla and ground ginger into a saucepan and warm through on a medium heat until a light simmer is reached. Take the pan off the heat and add the breadcrumbs and walnuts. Leave to stand for 10 minutes, then pour the filling into the tart case and bake for about 20 minutes, or until golden brown and bubbling around the sides.

Serve warm, with lashings of cold extra thick Jersey cream.

Makes 1 large tart, enough for 10
Not suitable for freezing whole, but you could freeze the cooked pastry case
Preparation time: 30 minutes, plus chilling time
Cooking time: 35 minutes, excluding pastry

FOR THE SWEET PASTRY
125g softened unsalted butter
80g caster sugar
10g soft light brown sugar
2 egg yolks
225g strong white bread flour, plus extra for dusting
a pinch of fine sea salt

FOR THE FILLING
600g golden syrup
finely grated zest and juice of ½ an orange
½ teaspoon vanilla extract
a pinch of ground ginger
175g fresh white breadcrumbs
100g walnuts, chopped small

SPICED PEPPER PLUM TART

Black pepper and plums go really well together. This might seem a lot of spicing, but it simply works brilliantly.

Slit the vanilla pod open lengthways and scrape out the seeds, discarding the pod. In an electric mixer with a beater attachment, or in a bowl with a wooden spoon, cream together the butter, both sugars, orange zest and vanilla seeds until light and fluffy. Add the egg yolks, one at a time, followed by the flour, spices, salt and baking powder and mix together slightly, then stop the machine and finish mixing by hand (you don't want to over-mix it). Just bring it all together on to a lightly floured surface and then divide into two-thirds for the bottom and one-third for the top.

Wrap each piece in baking paper, then put the larger piece into the fridge and the smaller piece into the freezer for at least 45 minutes.

Take the larger piece of pastry out of the fridge and leave for 30 minutes, or until you are able to roll it out.

Preheat the oven to 160°C/fan 140°C/gas 3 and grease and flour a 25cm loose-bottomed tart tin, 5–6cm deep.

Roll out the pastry on a lightly floured surface into a circle about 30cm across and 3mm thick, and line the prepared tart tin with it. Place the stoned and halved plums skin side down on the pastry and sprinkle them with about 2 teaspoons of caster sugar.

Now take the other piece of pastry out of the freezer. Using the large holes of a box grater, grate the pastry evenly over the plums until all are covered. Sprinkle with 2 tablespoons of demerara sugar, add a few twists of the pepper mill, then bake until golden brown – about 50–60 minutes.

Place on a rack to cool, still in the tin, and unmould when it has cooled for at least 20–30 minutes.

Serve warm, with extra thick Jersey cream.

Serves 8–12
Not suitable for freezing
Preparation time: 30 minutes, plus chilling time
Cooking time: 60 minutes

1 vanilla pod
250g softened unsalted butter
125g caster sugar, plus 2 teaspoons for sprinkling
125g demerara sugar, plus 2 tablespoons for sprinkling
finely grated zest of 1 orange
2 egg yolks
300g plain flour, plus extra for dusting
2 teaspoons ground mixed spice
1 teaspoon ground ginger
1 teaspoon ground allspice
½ teaspoon ground star anise
2 teaspoons ground black pepper, plus a few twists for the top
a pinch of ground cinnamon
a pinch of fine sea salt
1 teaspoon baking powder
600g plums, halved and stoned

COLD PUDDINGS

Creamy cold puddings are among my favourites – things like buttermilk pudding, so creamy and luxurious. Even an Eton mess, with broken meringue, fresh fruit and a little lightly whipped cream to bring it all together, is simple but delicious, and it's one of the best-selling puddings I used to make as a pastry chef.

The great thing with most of these puddings is that you can make them in advance. Working in restaurants, these were the backbone of the menu, as they meant you always had something up your sleeve ready to go – and the same is true for a home dinner party as well.

CREAM

One of the nicest things you can make in the pastry section is a pillow of lightly whipped sweetened vanilla cream, also known as crème Chantilly, to serve with puddings and to mix through desserts. Take care not to over-whip the cream, as it will split and then will not be nice at all. The cream should be silky smooth and just hold itself when you spoon it on to the plate.

CUSTARD

To make a bain-marie, or water bath, place your ramekins, dishes or moulds in a roasting pan or high-sided tray and fill the pan with hot water from the tap until it reaches halfway up the side of the ramekins or dishes. Cooking in the oven this way transfers the heat to the custard gently, preventing it from curdling or over-cooking. The steam that rises as the water heats also helps keep the top of the custard from getting a crust and going too dry.

GELATINE

I normally use a bronze leaf gelatine but it is quite hard to find (though there are some places that sell it online), and I have also added a powdered gelatine. The one I have been using is the Dr Oetker brand, which is available at most supermarkets. To use the powder, just whisk it into the warmed liquid and follow the recipe.

MERINGUES

Ideally you should use a machine for making meringues. There are a lot of old wives' tales about making them, but follow these steps and you will always have lovely meringues:

Always use double the weight of caster sugar to the weight of egg whites.

Using an electric mixer with a whisk attachment, whisk the egg whites on high speed till stiff peaks are reached, then turn down to a low speed and add all the sugar in one go. Turn back to a high speed and whisk until really thick, stiff and glossy.

Bake the meringues in a very low oven – try to bake them without any colour. The timing will depend on the size of your batch of egg whites (see page 250).

CIDER SYLLABUB

This gives enough cider mix to make this recipe twice, and the mix will keep happily for a year in a jar in the fridge. You will need some stewed or poached fruit to serve with the syllabub. It's fairly strong in cider, so take care ...

Mix together the cider, sherry, lemon zest and juice and pour into a jar – this will keep for ages in the fridge because of its high alcohol content.

To make the syllabub, pour half the cider mix into a mixing bowl (put the rest back into the fridge for another time). Add the sugar and cream and whisk to soft peaks.

Serve in martini glasses – place some of the stewed fruit at the bottom of each glass, then spoon the syllabub on top and chill in the fridge for 4 hours.

Just before serving, grate some nutmeg on top. Serve with tuile biscuits (see page 131).

Serves 6
Not suitable for freezing
Preparation time: 15 minutes
Chilling time: 4 hours

FOR THE CIDER MIX
240ml good still cider,
    e.g. Weston's
60ml sherry, e.g. amontillado
zest and juice of 1 lemon

FOR THE CREAM MIX
75g caster sugar
300ml double cream

TO SERVE
stewed or poached fruit,
    e.g. apples or plums
whole nutmeg, for grating

BLACKCURRANT LEAF CRÈME BRÛLÉE

You get a truly amazing flavour of blackcurrants from using the leaves, but be careful not to kill your plant by making this dish too many times in one year.

To make classic crème brûlée, omit the leaves and add 1 vanilla pod (slit it open lengthways, scrape out the seeds and add them to the cream and milk).

First, rip up the leaves and place them in a container. Pour in the milk and cream and leave overnight in the fridge.

Preheat the oven to 120°C/fan 100°C/gas ½.

Pour the milk mix into a heavy-based saucepan and slowly bring to the boil, stirring frequently. Meanwhile mix the egg yolks and sugar together in a large bowl for a minute or two. Once the milk mix is at scalding point, gradually pour it into the egg yolks, whisking all the time to prevent curdling. Leave to stand for 15 minutes, whisking every 5 minutes.

Pass through a fine sieve, then skim any foam off the top and pour into four 175ml heatproof moulds or ramekins. Stand the dishes in a water bath (see page 184) and bake for 45 minutes to 1 hour. You need to leave a wobble in the centre, as the residual heat will finish off the cooking and this way they will not over-cook. Take the brûlées out of the water bath and leave to cool, then put them into the fridge until cold (at least 4 hours or overnight).

Before serving, sprinkle 1 teaspoon of caster sugar over the top of each brûlée – just enough to cover the surface – then caramelize the sugar using a blowtorch or under a very hot grill.

Makes 4–5
Not suitable for freezing
Preparation time: 20 minutes, plus cooling time
Cooking time: 1 hour 10 minutes
Chilling time: overnight plus 4 hours

10 blackcurrant leaves
150ml full fat milk
400ml double cream
6 egg yolks
100g caster sugar
4 teaspoons caster sugar, for the top

BAKED SEVILLE CUSTARDS

Using bitter Seville oranges really makes these lovely custards. Ah, Seville oranges: not just for marmalade.

Preheat the oven to 140°C/fan 120°C/gas 1.

Finely zest 2 of the Seville oranges, then squeeze the juice from all 4 oranges and pour it into a jug. Stir in the brandy.

Pour the cream and milk into a heavy-based saucepan and bring to the boil. Meanwhile, whisk the eggs, egg yolks and both sugars together in a bowl for 2–3 minutes.

Once the cream is boiling, pour it into the egg mix, whisking all the time to prevent the eggs scrambling, then whisk in the Seville zest and juice and leave to stand for 5 minutes. Pass the mixture through a fine sieve, skim off any foam on top and pour into eight 175ml ramekins or small ovenproof dishes. Stand them in a water bath (see page 184) and bake for 40 minutes, or until just set.

You can serve the custards warm, with biscuits, or cool – chill them in the fridge, then sprinkle about 1 teaspoon of caster sugar over the top of each one (just enough to cover the surface) and caramelize with a blowtorch or under a very hot grill.

Makes 8
Not suitable for freezing
Preparation time: 20 minutes
Cooking time: 45 minutes
Chilling time, optional: 3–4 hours

4 Seville oranges, or large
   regular oranges
2 tablespoons brandy
500ml double cream
140ml full fat milk
4 eggs
4 egg yolks
120g caster sugar
60g demerara sugar
4 teaspoons caster sugar
   (optional), for the top

BAKED MALT CUSTARDS

Malt syrup comes from sprouted barley and the flavour can only be described as 'malty'. This is one of my favourite dishes, and has always had lots of praise from customers over the years. Malt syrup is available from most health food shops.

Preheat the oven to 120°C/fan 100°C/gas ½.

Put the egg yolks, malt syrup and both sugars into a large bowl and whisk together for 1 minute.

Put the cream into a heavy-based saucepan and bring to the boil. Pour the boiling cream into the egg yolk mix, whisking all the time to prevent curdling, then strain through a fine sieve into a large jug. Pour into four 250ml ramekins or ovenproof dishes and bake in a water bath (see page 184) for 40 minutes, or until just set. Take out of the water bath and leave to cool for half an hour, then chill in the fridge.

Serve with a biscuit of your choice (the chocolate and oat snaps on page 114 work well), or sprinkle some broken bits of honeycomb (see page 246) on top.

Makes 4
Not suitable for freezing
Preparation time: 20 minutes, plus chilling time
Cooking time: 40 minutes

6 egg yolks
70g malt syrup
65g caster sugar
10g soft light brown sugar
500ml double cream

JELLY
(WOBBLE FACTOR 9¾)

There's nothing as sexy as a good wobble on a jelly. I hate a very firm jell – follow this recipe to avoid a rubber-ball-like jelly.

Soak the gelatine leaves in cold water for about 10 minutes. Meanwhile, put 200ml of the juice into a saucepan and warm on the hob until hot, but not boiling.

Squeeze out the water from the gelatine leaves, pop them into the hot juice and whisk until dissolved. If using powdered gelatine, whisk it into the liquid. Then add the rest of the cold juice, pass through a fine sieve into a lightly oiled 600–800ml jelly mould or trifle bowl, and leave to set in the fridge.

Serve with hot madeleines (see page 44) and whipped cream.

Serves 4
Not suitable for freezing
Preparation time: 10 minutes
Chilling time: 6 hours or overnight

3 bronze gelatine leaves, or
  1 sachet (11g) of powdered
  gelatine
600ml sweetened fruit poaching
  liquid or juice

BUTTERMILK PUDDING

This pudding is like a panna cotta but is more giving, lighter and more mousse-like, with a wonderful creamy texture. If you can't get hold of buttermilk, Greek style yoghurt is great to use instead.

Soak the gelatine in cold water for about 8 minutes.

Peel the zest from the lemon in long pieces and squeeze the juice, then put into a saucepan with the sugar and half the cream. Slit the vanilla pod open lengthways and scrape out the seeds, then add the seeds and pod to the mixture. Place on a medium heat and slowly bring to the boil, stirring frequently. Turn down the heat and simmer for 4 minutes, then take off the heat.

Squeeze the water out of the gelatine leaves, add them to your heated cream mixture and whisk together until dissolved. If using powdered gelatine, whisk it into the liquid. Pass through a fine sieve into a bowl, removing and discarding the lemon peel and vanilla pod.

Add the buttermilk to the sieved mixture and whisk together briefly, using a balloon whisk.

In a different bowl, whisk the remaining half of the cream to soft peaks. Add it to the buttermilk mixture and gently whisk together until you can't see any lumps. Pour into eight 175–200ml moulds or ramekins and put into the fridge to set for 4–5 hours.

Serve with ginger snaps (see page 136), and fresh strawberries or poached rhubarb (remember to keep the juice for jellies).

Serves 8
Not suitable for freezing
Preparation time: 20 minutes
Cooking time: 10 minutes
Chilling time: 4–5 hours

3 bronze gelatine leaves, or 1 sachet (11g) of powdered gelatine
1 lemon
250g caster sugar
400ml double cream
1 vanilla pod
600ml buttermilk

REGENT'S PARK HONEY MOUSSE

These mousses are like eating sweet clouds of joy. Regent's Park honey is available from www.purefood.co.uk – it has a lovely floral flavour and changes from season to season. If you can't get hold of it, you can use another floral honey such as orange blossom.

First whip the double cream, soured cream and Armagnac syrup together in a bowl until you have soft peaks. Place in the fridge to chill.

Next you need to make an Italian meringue. Put the honey and glucose into a heavy-based saucepan and bring to the boil. Meanwhile, in an electric mixer with a whisk attachment, whisk up the egg whites to stiff peaks, then slowly pour in the boiling honey while the machine is on slow speed. Once all the honey has been added, turn the mixer up to high speed and whip until cool.

Add the crème patissière to the whipped cream and whisk together until thickened, then fold in the meringue.

Spoon into 150ml moulds or ramekins and leave to set in the fridge for about 3–4 hours. Alternatively you can freeze them to make frozen honey mousses, as the sweetness stops them setting too hard.

Serve with lots of fresh raspberries or some Armagnac prunes and a few orange biscuits (see page 132).

Serves 6

Suitable for freezing
(for a few days)

Preparation time: 20 minutes
(excluding the crème patissière)

Cooking time: 5 minutes

Chilling time: 3–4 hours

50ml double cream

50ml soured cream

1 tablespoon Armagnac syrup
(from the prunes in
Armagnac on page 240)

80g Regent's Park honey
(or other floral honey)

40ml liquid glucose

2 egg whites

200g crème patissière
(see page 146)

CHOCOLATE TERRINE

This dessert is a great one to pull out of the bag for a large dinner party, as it's really easy to make the day before, looks amazing, and hey, most people love chocolate. Try to use the best dark chocolate you can.

Serves 14–16
Suitable for freezing
Preparation time: 25 minutes
Cooking time: 5 minutes
Chilling time: overnight

115g dark chocolate (70%)
225g unsalted butter
5 egg yolks
115g caster sugar
90g cocoa powder (100%), sifted
a pinch of fine sea salt
340ml double cream
35g icing sugar, sifted

Line the inside of a terrine mould measuring 25cm x 8cm x 8cm with clingfilm.

Chop your chocolate carefully into small pieces and put it into a large bowl with the butter. Stand the bowl over a saucepan of simmering water and let the chocolate mixture melt slowly.

While the chocolate and butter are melting, put your egg yolks and sugar into a bowl and whisk together until white and fluffy (which should take about 5 minutes).

Whisk in the sifted cocoa powder and salt – the mixture will become quite stiff – then put to one side.

Pour the cream into a heavy-based saucepan, add the sifted icing sugar and slowly bring to the boil.

Add your melted chocolate mixture to the egg yolks, whisking all the time to prevent lumps (you can sieve it later if you do get any, though, so don't worry too much). It should be like a thick chocolate paste.

Now take your pan of boiling cream off the heat and slowly add to your chocolate paste. Be very careful of the hot cream – it must be just off the boil, as it's the heat from the cream which will set the terrine.

When all mixed in, it will be smooth and glossy – if there are still any lumps, just pass it through a fine sieve. Pour into your prepared terrine mould and put into the fridge overnight to set.

To serve, unmould the terrine and remove the clingfilm. Then, using a long thin sharp kitchen knife, slice it into thin slices, place on the plate and just run a blowtorch, if you have one, over the slice to shine the chocolate and give it the wow factor. Serve with fresh cherries, crème fraîche and ginger snaps (see page 136) or chocolate and oat snaps (see page 114).

CHOCOLATE CARAMEL BRANDY CREAMS

The caramel and brandy add a lovely depth of flavour.

First put the caster sugar into a medium heavy-based saucepan and place over a medium heat. Give it a little stir every now and then until the sugar melts and turns to a golden caramel. You want it fairly dark, so once it has reached this point remove the pan from the heat and add 100ml of the cream so it doesn't over-cook – watch out, though, as it will spit a bit and boil furiously. Put the pan back on a low heat to dissolve the caramel into the cream, which should only take about 1–2 minutes, then set aside to cool down.

Melt the chocolate in a bowl over a pan of simmering water. Once melted, whisk in the egg yolks one at a time, then whisk in the caramel mix and leave to cool.

In a separate large bowl, whisk up the rest of the cream to soft peaks. Fold in the chocolate mixture, followed by the brandy, then pour into six 150ml ramekins or dishes and leave to set in the fridge for 2 hours. Try not to leave them in for too long, as you don't want them to set too much.

Serve slightly chilled, with nutters or orange biscuits (see pages 128 and 132).

Makes 6
Not suitable for freezing
Preparation time: 15 minutes
Cooking time: 10 minutes
Chilling time: 2 hours

150g caster sugar
475ml double cream
175g dark chocolate (70%),
    broken into pieces
7 egg yolks
a very generous glug of brandy

CHOCOLATE POTS

These intense little pots of joy are suited to any moment: lunch, dinner or a late-night treat.

Put all the chopped chocolate into a large mixing bowl – if you are not using buttons it will need to be chopped up into small pieces.

Put the egg yolks and sifted icing sugar into another bowl and mix together for about a minute.

Heat the milk and cream in a medium saucepan on a medium heat, stirring occasionally until it comes to scalding point, then gradually pour it over your egg yolk mixture, whisking all the time to prevent curdling. Immediately pour through a sieve into the bowl of chocolate, whisking as the residual heat melts the chocolate, then add the pinch of salt and whisk in.

Once melted together, cool to room temperature, whisking occasionally for about 20 minutes, then pour carefully into eight 175ml glasses or ramekins, leaving a little room on top.

You can serve them warm or chill them for a few hours in the fridge. Serve with a tablespoon of pouring cream on top, and with chocolate and oat biscuits (see page 114).

Makes about 8
Not suitable for freezing
Preparation time: 30 minutes

350g dark chocolate (70%), chopped
100g dark chocolate (100%, or as near as you can get), chopped
5 egg yolks
100g icing sugar, sifted
600ml full fat milk
300ml double cream
a pinch of fine sea salt
8 tablespoons single cream

CUSTARD TART

What can I say about my custard tart ... how about HEAVENLY!
I have had a few marriage proposals as a result of this dessert. The
most useful piece of advice I can impart is to let your pastry case get
a little browner than you think it should be at the blind baking stage.

Put the butter and sugars into the bowl of an electric mixer with a
beater attachment and cream together until white and fluffy. Add the
egg yolks one at a time to help prevent them curdling, then sift in the
flour and salt and and mix until all is incorporated. Turn out on to a
lightly floured surface and bring together, then wrap in clingfilm and
chill in the fridge for 5–6 hours.

Grease and flour a 30cm tart tin, 3–4 cm deep. Take the pastry
out of the fridge and allow it to soften a little. Roll it out on a lightly
floured surface to a circle about 35cm across and about 3mm thick,
and line your prepared tart case with it. Chill for 2–3 hours in the
fridge or 45 minutes in the freezer.

Preheat the oven to 160°C/ fan 140°C/gas 3.

Take the tart case straight from the fridge or freezer, cover it with
clingfilm and fill with baking beans, then bake for 25 minutes, or until
the edges are golden brown. Remove the clingfilm and beans, then put
the tart case back into the oven and bake for a further 8–10 minutes,
or until it is golden brown all over (do not under-bake the tart case
otherwise you will have a soggy bottom).

Remove the tart case from the oven and brush with beaten egg
yolk (this seals any holes), then place on a rack still in the tin and cool
the pastry completely.

Preheat the oven to 140°C/fan 120°C/gas 1.

Slit the vanilla pod lengthways and scrape out the seeds. Put the
seeds and pod into a saucepan with the double cream and bring
slowly to the boil, to infuse the cream with the vanilla.

In a large bowl, whisk the egg yolks and sugar together just for a
minute. Pour the boiling cream over the mixture, whisking constantly
to prevent curdling. Pass through a fine sieve. If there is lots of froth
on top, just spoon it off and discard.

Serves 10–12
Not suitable for freezing
Preparation time: 40 minutes,
    plus chilling time
Cooking time: 1 hour 5 minutes

FOR THE SWEET PASTRY
250g softened unsalted butter
160g caster sugar
20g soft light brown sugar
4 egg yolks, plus 1 yolk
    for brushing
450g strong white bread flour
a pinch of fine sea salt

FOR THE FILLING
1 vanilla pod
800ml double cream
9 egg yolks
100g caster sugar
1 whole nutmeg, for grating

Pour the warm custard mix into the blind-baked tart case, then grate the nutmeg on top (do not use ready-ground nutmeg). Place carefully in the oven without spilling any of it down the sides of the pastry case; if you do, you will end up with soggy pastry, which is a no-no for a custard tart.

Bake for about 40 minutes, or until there is only a small wobble in the centre of the tart.

Take out of the oven and place on a rack to cool. Leave in the tin until cooled completely, then turn out.

Best eaten on the day it's made, and at its absolute best when eaten within 2 hours of making.

THE CHOCOLATE BROWNIE

I started making this brownie shortly after starting at St John Restaurant in 2000, and have been following the recipe ever since. It's a favourite of many customers and chefs alike.

Preheat the oven to 180°C/fan 160°C/gas 4. Line and lightly grease a 36cm x 26cm x 3.5cm baking tray.

Put the almonds and hazelnuts into a roasting tin and roast them for about 10–15 minutes, stirring them every few minutes until they are golden brown. Leave them to cool, then chop them roughly.

Put the butter and 400g of the chocolate into a heatproof bowl over a pan of lightly simmering water and leave to melt slowly.

While the chocolate is melting, mix the eggs and sugar together in a large bowl, using a wooden spoon and mixing just enough to combine. Once melted, pour the chocolate mix into the egg mix and whisk together briefly. Fold in the nuts and the rest of the chocolate, then sift in the flour and salt and fold into the mix.

Pour the mixture into the prepared baking tray and bake for 25 minutes. Take out of the oven and put the tray on a cooling rack for 1 hour (it might look a little under-baked, but as it cools it will firm up).

Serve warm, for a moist brownie, or chill in the fridge overnight, which I prefer. Either way, serve with vanilla ice cream and a caramel chocolate sauce (see page 248).

Makes enough for 16 large brownies
Preparation time: 25 minutes
Cooking time: 25 minutes

160g whole blanched almonds
160g whole blanched hazelnuts
300g unsalted butter, chopped
500g Valrhona or other dark
    chocolate (70%), broken or
    chopped into small pieces
5 eggs
500g caster sugar
100g plain flour
a pinch of fine sea salt

HAZELNUT AND RASPBERRY ROLL

A really nice pudding for the summer – delicious made with raspberries, but you can equally well use strawberries or a mix of summer berries. Great for a picnic or after a barbecue, good on a buffet table, or even as a birthday cake. It looks amazing and no one will be able to resist it.

Serves 8
Not suitable for freezing
Preparation time: 30 minutes
Cooking time: 20 minutes

100g blanched hazelnuts
360g cream cheese
20g icing sugar, sifted
4 eggs, separated
110g caster sugar, plus
   2 tablespoons for sprinkling
50g hazelnut praline, plus extra
   for sprinkling (see page 247)
75g raspberry jam (see page 241)
100g fresh raspberries, plus extra
   for garnish
150ml whipping cream

Preheat the oven to 180°C/fan 160°C/gas 4. Grease a 33cm × 23cm Swiss roll tin and line it with baking paper.

Put the nuts into a small roasting tin and toast in the oven for 10–12 minutes, until golden brown. Leave them to get cold, then whiz them to fine crumbs in a food processor.

To make the filling, beat the cream cheese and icing sugar together until smooth. Put into the fridge to chill.

Using an electric mixer with a whisk attachment, whisk the egg yolks and caster sugar on high speed for 4 minutes, then scrape out into another bowl. Whisk the egg whites to soft peaks (you don't want to over-whisk here). Gently fold the whizzed-up hazelnuts and hazelnut praline into the egg yolks, then carefully fold in the egg whites.

Pour into your prepared Swiss roll tin and bake for 8 minutes, or until golden brown and springy to the touch.

Take out of the oven and pour 25ml water underneath the baking paper (the steam will help release the roll from the paper). Invert the sponge on to a sheet of baking paper sprinkled with the extra 2 tablespoons of caster sugar. Watch out that you don't get any water on the roll and remove the paper carefully.

Leave to cool for a few minutes, then spread all the cream cheese filling over the surface of the Swiss roll. Soften the jam slightly by spooning it into a small bowl and stirring it, then spoon it on top of the filling and gently spread it over with a small palette knife. Sprinkle some of the fresh raspberries over the jam.

Roll up the filled sponge fairly tightly from the long side then wrap it in greaseproof paper, twisting the ends of the paper tightly. Leave to cool.

When ready to serve, whisk the cream in a bowl until fairly stiff and spoon into a piping bag fitted with a star nozzle. Unwrap the roll and place it on a plate. Pipe whipped cream on top, down the centre. Place fresh raspberries on top and sprinkle with a little more hazelnut praline.

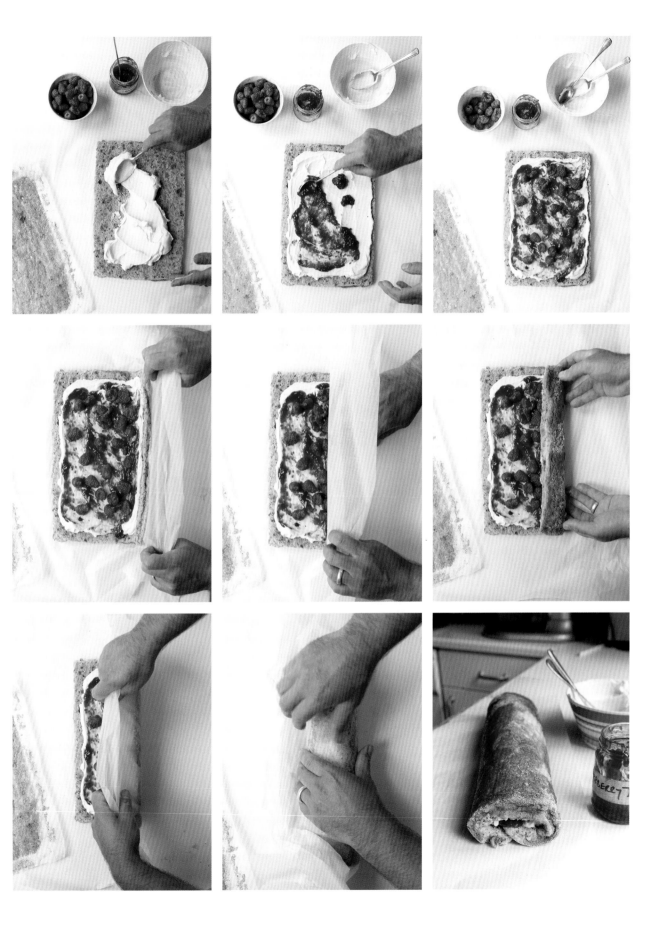

TRIFLE WITH JELLY

I usually use fruit compote when I make a trifle, but this intense jelly has a good wobble factor and works perfectly here.

First make the juice for the jelly. Chop the rhubarb into 2.5cm sticks and pop into a non-metallic bowl. Add the sugar, water, orange rind and juice and mix together well. Cover and leave overnight at room temperature to let the juices from the rhubarb seep out.

Preheat the oven to 140°C/fan 120°C/gas 1.

Put the rhubarb mix into a deep ovenproof lidded saucepan or casserole. Place it in the oven with the lid on and bake for about 40 minutes, or until the rhubarb has softened.

Once cooked, take out of the oven, then thickly slice the strawberries and add them to the rhubarb. Put the lid back on and leave to cool, then strain the juice through a fine sieve and put to one side.

Turn the oven up to 160°C/fan 140°C/gas 3. Lightly grease and line a 20cm square loose-bottomed tin.

Next make the sponge (you will only need half, but the sponge freezes very well – it can also be used in the apple pie recipe on page 172). In an electric mixer with a whisk attachment, whisk the eggs and sugar together until light and fluffy. This will take about 3–4 minutes on high speed. While the eggs and sugar are mixing, melt the butter on a low heat and put to one side. When the egg mix is light and fluffy, stop the machine and remove the bowl, then add the sifted flour and slowly fold in until all is incorporated. Pour in the warm melted butter and again fold in slowly until all is incorporated.

Pour the mix into the prepared cake tin and bake for 25–30 minutes, or until golden brown and firm to the touch. Once baked, take out of the oven and leave in the tin for 5 minutes before turning out on to a rack to cool.

Now the custard: split the vanilla pod lengthways and scrape out the seeds. Put pod and seeds into a saucepan with the double cream and slowly bring to the boil. At the same time put a small pan of water on to the heat and bring to a slow simmer.

In a heatproof bowl large enough to fit over the saucepan of simmering water, mix the eggs, egg yolks and sugar together for 2 minutes. Once the cream is at scalding point, pour it into the egg mix, whisking all the time to prevent the eggs scrambling, then place the bowl over the pan of simmering water, whisking from time to time until the custard has thickened – this

»

Serves 10–12
Not suitable for freezing
Preparation time: 1½ hours
  (excluding the honeycomb)
Cooking time: 1 hour 30 minutes
  (excluding the honeycomb)
Chilling time: overnight, plus
  a few hours

FOR THE SPONGE
5 eggs
150g caster sugar
60g unsalted butter
150g plain flour, sifted

FOR THE CUSTARD
1 vanilla pod
450ml double cream
2 eggs
2 egg yolks
85g caster sugar

FOR THE FRUIT AND JELLY
800g rhubarb, trimmed
150g caster sugar
400ml water
4 strips of orange rind
juice of 1 orange
125g strawberries, hulled
4½ bronze gelatine leaves or 1½
  sachets of powdered gelatine

FOR THE SUGARED ALMONDS
50g almonds
15g icing sugar, sifted
1 tablespoon brandy

will take 10–15 minutes of continuous stirring. To test whether the custard is thick enough, just put a little on to a cold plate and pop it into the freezer for 1 minute to see if it sets.

Pass the custard through a fine sieve into a large jug, discarding the vanilla pod, and put to one side to cool for 5 minutes. Place a piece of clingfilm directly on the surface of the custard to prevent a skin from forming. Cool to room temperature, then place in the fridge for at least 2 hours, until needed.

For the nuts: preheat the oven to 160°C/fan 140°C/gas 3. Mix the almonds, icing sugar and brandy together in a bowl. Sprinkle them on a lined baking tray and toast in the oven for 8–10 minutes, or until golden brown (watch out as nuts are easy to burn), then leave to cool.

Now to build the masterpiece:

First the sponge: take half the sponge and cut it into slices 2.5cm thick, then cut each slice into quarters. Place evenly over the bottom of a glass bowl about 23cm wide and 10cm deep, then pour on the booze. The quantity is up to the chef's discretion but I would say not too much more than 3 tablespoons, otherwise the sponge may be too soggy. Leave for 30 minutes to soak in, then squeeze down the sponge so it's just at the bottom of the bowl.

Now the jelly: strain the rhubarb, discarding the strips of orange rind, and measure the juice. You should have about 900ml – if not, top it up with water or orange juice. Soak the gelatine leaves in cold water for about 10 minutes. While the gelatine is soaking, warm 150ml of the juice on the stove until hot. Squeeze out the water from the gelatine, then pop it into the hot juice and whisk until dissolved. If using powdered gelatine, whisk it into the liquid. Add the rest of the juice and pass through a fine sieve. Lay the poached rhubarb and strawberries on top of the sponge and gently pour over the jelly juice. Put into the fridge until the jelly has set – about 3–4 hours, or overnight.

Once set, take out of the fridge and gently pour over the custard. Put back into the fridge until set – at least 2 hours.

When ready to serve, whip the cream, vanilla and icing sugar together until soft peaks are reached and either pipe or spoon it on evenly. Sprinkle with sugared violets, diced strawberries, sugared almonds, honeycomb and sprigs of mint.

Enjoy.

TO DECORATE
3 strawberries, diced small
1 tablespoon sugared violets
25g honeycomb (see page 246)
3–4 sprigs of fresh mint

FOR THE BOOZE
3 tablespoons sweet sherry
  or golden rum

FOR THE WHIPPED CREAM
450ml double cream
1 teaspoon vanilla extract
60g icing sugar

BLOOD ORANGE POSSET

This is one of the simplest puddings to put together – the flavour and texture give it a soothing quality and it is also a light pudding to serve after a heavy meal. If blood oranges are not in season you can just use normal oranges or lemons instead, increasing the sugar to 150g if you make a lemon posset.

Serves 5
Not suitable for freezing
Preparation time: 15 minutes
Cooking time: 5 minutes
Chilling time: at least 4 hours

2 blood oranges
1 lemon
500ml double cream
120g caster sugar
1 vanilla pod

First zest the oranges – you will need 1 teaspoon of zest. Now squeeze the juice from the oranges and the lemon, keeping the zest and juice separate.

Pour the cream into a heavy-based saucepan and add the sugar. Slit the vanilla pod open lengthways and scrape out the seeds, then put pod and seeds into the pan. Place on a low heat and add the zest.

Slowly bring to the boil, then turn down to a light simmer for about 2 minutes (this is to infuse the vanilla and to draw out the oils from the zest). Remove from the heat and whisk in the orange and lemon juice, then pass through a fine sieve into a large jug.

Pour into five 250ml moulds or ramekins – when I make these I whisk the mixture just before I pour it into each mould, as this makes for a little bit of a lighter top layer and also looks good.

Chill in the fridge for about 4 hours.

Serve with biscuits such as butter fingers (see page 134).

CRUNCH IN THE MOUTH

Does exactly what it says on the tin. These are really good for big parties, served like dessert canapés on trays.

To make the profiteroles, put the butter, water and sugar into a medium heavy-based saucepan and bring to the boil. Once the butter has melted and the water is boiling, take off the heat and stir in the sifted flour and salt. Put back on the heat and cook for about 2–3 minutes, until the paste leaves the sides of the saucepan easily, then take off the heat and cool.

Beat in the eggs one at a time until all are incorporated, then let the mixture rest for 30 minutes.

Preheat the oven to 180°C/fan 160°C/gas 4. Line a large baking tray or two smaller ones with baking paper.

Prepare a large piping bag fitted with a plain 1.5cm nozzle and fill the bag with the pastry mix. On your prepared trays pipe thirty rounds about 3cm across and about 20g each, leaving space between them as they will spread a little and to help them bake evenly. Bake for 25 minutes, until risen and golden brown, then take out of the oven and place on a rack to cool.

Now make the caramel. Prepare a water bath by filling the sink a third of the way up with very cold water or with some ice cubes. Put all the ingredients into a large, very clean, heavy-based saucepan, place on a low heat, and melt the sugar and glucose together. Once melted, turn the heat up to high and bring up the temperature to 160°C on a digital thermometer – making sure the reading is from the middle of the caramel and not the bottom of the saucepan. Place the saucepan immediately in your cold water bath for 1–2 minutes to stop the caramel colouring any further. Watch out as you put the saucepan in the water bath, as it will spit boiling water around.

Line another baking tray with baking paper. Dip each of your profiteroles into the caramel and lay them on the baking tray caramel side down. Leave to cool and harden.

Once hard, slice your profiteroles in half and fill with your desired filling. Serve with hot chocolate and caramel sauce.

Makes about 30
Not suitable for freezing
Preparation time: 25 minutes
(excluding ice cream, sauce
and crème patissière)
Cooking time: 35 minutes

FOR THE PROFITEROLES
100g unsalted butter
250ml water
5g caster sugar
140g plain flour, sifted
a pinch of fine sea salt
4 eggs

FOR THE CARAMEL
500g granulated sugar
165ml water
65ml liquid glucose

FOR THE FILLINGS
vanilla ice cream (see page 216)
crème patissière (see page 146)
chocolate and caramel sauce
(see page 248), to serve

ICE CREAM

One of my first loves as a child was the Mr Whippy 99 (with flake).
I used to listen out for the chimes of the ice cream van and run down
the street with my brother and sister to catch it. Luckily we still have
a van which comes to our street in Norwood during the summer, but
now I've grown up I do like an 'Oyster'. My favourite place to get ice
cream in London now is from Kitty at La Grotta Ices.

The great thing about ice cream is that it's made in advance, so
you don't have to worry about it – but don't forget to take out the
hard-set ones about 5 minutes before scooping, so that they have
time to soften a little.

Ice cream makes a pretty much instant dessert, but it's nice to serve it
with a crunchy biscuit or put it into a cone. Make sure you always have a
tub or two of vanilla ice cream in the freezer, as it is the perfect garnish
for many puddings.

At the St John Hotel in Chinatown we made amazing sundaes in glass
dishes for dessert, which you can easily recreate with the recipes in
this chapter: try using one ice cream, one sorbet, a pillow of whipped
cream, some fresh fruit to complement one of the ices, a biscuit, some
toasted almonds and some sauce from the fresh fruit.

Here's one idea for what you can put in a sundae, to get you started:

STRAWBERRY AND
BLACK PEPPER SUNDAE

1 scoop of strawberry sorbet (see page 237)

1 scoop of black pepper ice cream (see page 219)

1 pillow of whipped cream

3 strawberries, sliced

3 strawberries, whizzed up for sauce

sugared almonds (see page 207)

2 tuile biscuits or ginger snaps (see pages 131 and 136)

icing sugar, to dust

EQUIPMENT AND TIPS

It is really useful to have an ice cream machine: Cuisinart, Kenwood and Magimix all make good ones for a range of prices, and you can even get an attachment for the KitchenAid mixer. Some have a built-in compressor for automatic freezing or an insulated bowl that requires freezing. If using the latter, remember to freeze the bowl the night before you want to make the ice cream.

Best results will be given by chilling completely, then churning in your ice cream machine, whichever type you have. Churning will take about 20–30 minutes, but you should refer to the manufacturer's instructions.

I would recommend that you go for one with a built-in freezer if you intend to make lots of ice cream, but if you don't have an ice cream machine it is possible to make it by hand, following this method:

Every 2–3 hours, take the mixture out of the freezer and give it a stir. Once it is softly set, beat it well with electric beaters, then freeze solid.

If the batch is too large for your machine, you can freeze the remainder using the by-hand method above, or leave the remainder of the batch overnight in the fridge to allow the ice cream bowl time to re-freeze.

While chilling, cover the surface of the mixture to prevent a skin from forming.

I use golden caster sugar for all the recipes in this chapter except for the caramel in the praline and the stock syrup.

I use large egg yolks for all the ice cream recipes. Egg whites can be used for other recipes (see meringues, page 250) and will freeze successfully.

The ice creams and sorbets will keep in the freezer for approximately 3 months.

VANILLA ICE CREAM

The classic: you should always have a tub or two in your freezer for barbecues, dinner parties or just a night in front of the TV. It's great to serve with most puddings, for example an apple pie or a lovely wobbly jelly, it's always good on its own or with chocolate and caramel sauce (see page 248) – and the kids love it.

Makes about 1 litre
Preparation time: 10 minutes,
   plus chilling and freezing
Cooking time: 20 minutes

375ml full fat milk
450ml double cream
2 vanilla pods
5 egg yolks (keep the whites
   for meringues, see page 250)
150g caster sugar

Pour the milk and cream into a heavy-based saucepan. Split the vanilla pods lengthways and scrape out the seeds, then add both pods and seeds to the pan.

On a medium heat, slowly bring to a gentle simmer and keep simmering for 3 minutes, to draw the oils out of the vanilla.

Meanwhile put your egg yolks and sugar into a large bowl and mix together.

After 3 minutes' simmering, turn up the heat under the milk and bring just to the boil. Pour into the egg yolks, whisking constantly to prevent the eggs from curdling.

Pour back into the saucepan and cook the custard on a low heat, stirring all the time, until it can coat the back of a spoon. This will take approximately 10 minutes. Do not allow the custard to boil or you will end up with scrambled eggs.

Strain through a fine sieve into a bowl, discarding the vanilla pods, and chill in an ice bath, made by filling a larger bowl one-third full with ice and water. Stir occasionally to stop a skin forming. When it's cold, lay a piece of clingfilm directly on the surface of the custard and place in the fridge to chill until completely cold, or churn straight away in your ice cream machine. Churn according to the manufacturer's instructions, then transfer to a freezer-proof container and freeze until solid.

Serve the ice cream on its own or with caramel and chocolate sauce (see page 248) or goat's milk caramel (see page 249). Before serving, take it out of the freezer for about 10–15 minutes to allow it to soften.

RECIPES USING THE VANILLA ICE CREAM BASE

You can make a big batch of vanilla ice cream, split it into four, and make vanilla ice cream and three other flavours. My favourite ice cream has got to be my rum and raisin – it's a bit boozy but it's smooth and creamy, and I love it.

Where no quantities are given, add them according to taste.

All ingredients are strained and discarded, apart from fennel, tarragon and bay leaves.

BAY LEAF ICE CREAM – add 6 crushed bay leaves to the milk and cream and leave out the vanilla. Great to serve with apple desserts.

RHUBARB RIPPLE – churn the vanilla as normal, then ripple the rhubarb jam (see page 242) through the churned ice cream. Lovely in a cone.

HONEYCOMB (see page 246) – churn the vanilla as normal, then add crushed honeycomb to the churned ice cream. Great on its own or as part of an ice cream sundae.

BLACK PEPPER – once strained, add 1½ teaspoons of freshly ground black pepper to the vanilla base, then chill it. Serve with strawberries and in a sundae.

TARRAGON – leave out the vanilla and add 4 tablespoons of chopped tarragon to the milk and cream, including the stalks (which contain lots of flavour). Another ice cream that's lovely with strawberries.

Top, left to right: black pepper, honeycomb, liquorice

Middle, left to right: lemon meringue, tarragon, rhubarb ripple

Bottom, left to right: fennel blossom, blackberry and crème fraîche, brown sugar and hazelnut

LIQUORICE – add 100g sliced thin liquorice bars to the milk and cream with the vanilla, making sure the liquorice has dissolved before you pour it over the egg yolks. Nice to serve with pear or apple desserts.

BUTTERSCOTCH CRUNCH (see page 245) – churn the vanilla as normal, then add small broken pieces of butterscotch to the churned ice cream and leave overnight to freeze, as this will soften the butterscotch a little. Great on its own.

LEMON MERINGUE – add the zest of 1 lemon to the milk with the vanilla. Churn as normal. Then add broken pieces of meringue (see page 250) and ripple some lemon curd (see page 244) through. Serve with a few cheeky raspberries.

RUM AND RAISIN (see page 240) – once strained, add 8 tablespoons of rum-soaked raisins to the vanilla base, then freeze. My favourite. Serve it on its own.

FENNEL BLOSSOM – use only 1 vanilla pod, and add 6 tablespoons of fennel blossom/fennel fronds and 2 tablespoons of crushed fennel seeds to the milk and vanilla. Once strained, add 2 tablespoons of Pernod and a pinch of salt, then freeze. Lovely with really ripe peaches or nectarines.

BLACKBERRY AND CRÈME FRAÎCHE ICE CREAM

This is a good one for all you urban foragers – get out there and pick your own wild blackberries. You get a wonderful vibrant purple fruitiness from the blackberries and a pleasant acidic note from the crème fraîche. Great served just on its own.

Makes about 1.3 litres
Preparation time: 10 minutes,
    plus chilling and freezing
Cooking time: 20 minutes

460g blackberries
330ml full fat milk
6 egg yolks
250g caster sugar
330ml crème fraîche

First whiz up the blackberries in a food processor and put to one side. Pour the milk into a heavy-based saucepan and bring slowly to the boil. Put the egg yolks and sugar into a large bowl and mix together. When the milk is just boiling, pour it over the egg yolks, whisking constantly to prevent the eggs from curdling.

Pour back into the saucepan and cook the custard on a low heat, stirring all the time, until it can coat the back of a spoon. This will take approximately 10 minutes. Do not allow the custard to boil or you will end up with scrambled eggs.

Strain through a fine sieve, then whisk in the blackberries and crème fraîche. Chill in an ice bath, made by filling a larger bowl one-third full with ice and water. Stir occasionally to stop a skin forming. When it's cold, lay a piece of clingfilm directly on the surface of the custard and place in the fridge until completely cold, or churn straight away in your ice cream machine. Churn according to the manufacturer's instructions then transfer to a freezer-proof container and freeze until solid.

To make the ice cream by hand, take the mixture out of the freezer every 2–3 hours and give it a stir. Once it is softly set, beat it well with electric beaters, then freeze solid.

BROWN SUGAR AND HAZELNUT ICE CREAM

I love this ice cream – it has a delicious flavour from the praline and a nice texture from the nuts. Great to serve on its own, in a cone or as part of a sundae.

Makes about 1.3 litres
Preparation time: 10 minutes,
   plus chilling and freezing
Cooking time: 20 minutes

500ml full fat milk
600ml double cream
6 egg yolks
100g soft dark brown sugar
100g soft light brown sugar
125g hazelnut praline
   (see page 247)

Pour the milk and cream into a heavy-based saucepan and slowly bring to the boil.

Put the egg yolks and both sugars into a large bowl and mix together. When the milk is just boiling, pour it into the egg yolks, whisking constantly to prevent the eggs from curdling.

Pour back into the saucepan and cook the custard on a low heat, stirring all the time, until it can coat the back of a spoon. This will take approximately 10 minutes. Do not allow the custard to boil or you will end up with scrambled eggs.

Strain through a fine sieve, then chill in an ice bath, made by filling a larger bowl one-third full with ice and water. Stir occasionally to stop a skin forming. When it's cold, lay a piece of clingfilm directly on the surface of the custard and place in the fridge until completely cold, or churn straight away in your ice cream machine. Churn according to the manufacturer's instructions. Once churned, stir in the hazelnut praline, transfer to a freezer-proof container and freeze until solid.

To make the ice cream by hand, take the mixture out of the freezer every 2–3 hours and give it a stir. Once it is softly set, beat it well with electric beaters, then freeze solid.

ORANGE AND CARDAMOM ICE CREAM

This creamy ice has an unusual twist to the flavour from the cardamom but it works really well with the orange. You won't be disappointed.

Makes about 1.5 litres
Preparation time: 10 minutes,
    plus chilling and freezing
Cooking time: 20 minutes

550ml freshly squeezed orange juice
    or good bought orange juice
4 teaspoons crushed cardamom
    pods
550ml full milk
550ml double cream
8 egg yolks
225g caster sugar

Pour the orange juice into a saucepan and place on a high heat until it has reduced by half (this will take about 5–10 minutes). Take off the heat and leave to cool.

Shell the cardamoms and crush the seeds in a pestle and mortar or a spice/coffee grinder.

Pour the milk and cream into a heavy-based saucepan, add the crushed cardamom, and bring slowly to the boil.

Put the egg yolks and sugar into a large bowl and mix together. When the milk is just boiling, pour it into the egg yolk mix, whisking constantly to prevent the eggs from curdling.

Pour back into the saucepan and cook the custard on a low heat, stirring all the time, until it can coat the back of a spoon. This will take approximately 10 minutes. Do not allow the custard to boil or you will end up with scrambled eggs.

Now add the orange juice. Strain through a fine sieve, then chill in an ice bath, made by filling a larger bowl one-third full with ice and water. Stir occasionally to stop a skin forming. When it's cold, lay a piece of clingfilm directly on the surface of the custard and place in the fridge until completely cold, or churn straight away in your ice cream machine. Churn according to the manufacturer's instructions, then transfer to a freezer-proof container and freeze until solid.

To make the ice cream by hand, take the mixture out of the freezer every 2–3 hours and give it a stir. Once it is softly set, beat it well with electric beaters, then freeze solid.

CHOCOLATE, VANILLA AND MALT ICE CREAM

This is like a really, really creamy cold Malteser. Malt extract is available from some supermarkets and health food shops.

Put the Horlicks into a small bowl and stir in a little of the milk to make a paste. Pour the rest of the milk and the cream into a heavy-based saucepan. Split the vanilla pod lengthways and scrape out the seeds, then add both pod and seeds to the pan with the malt extract and the Horlicks paste.

Put the pan on a medium heat, stirring to dissolve the malt and Horlicks, and slowly bring to a light simmer. Continue to simmer for 4 minutes, to draw the oils out of the vanilla and bring out the flavour of the malt.

Meanwhile, put the egg yolks and sugar into a large bowl and mix together. Once the milk has simmered for 4 minutes, turn up the heat and bring it just to the boil. Pour it into the egg yolks, whisking constantly to prevent the eggs from curdling.

Pour back into the saucepan and cook the custard on a low heat, stirring all the time, until it can coat the back of a spoon. This will take approximately 10 minutes. Do not allow the custard to boil or you will end up with scrambled eggs.

Strain through a fine sieve into a bowl, discarding the vanilla pod, then add the chocolate and salt to the custard and stir until melted. Chill in an ice bath, made by filling a larger bowl one-third full with ice and water. Stir occasionally to stop a skin forming. When it's cool, lay a piece of clingfilm directly on the surface of the custard and leave until it's completely cold.

Churn in your ice cream machine, according to the manufacturer's instructions. To make the ice cream by hand, take the mixture out of the freezer every 2–3 hours and give it a stir. Once it is softly set, beat it well with electric beaters, then freeze solid.

It's best to serve this ice cream straight away after it's churned, as it does set quite hard. If you make it by hand, take it out of the freezer a few minutes before you want to serve it, to give it time to soften slightly.

Makes about 1 litre
Preparation time: 10 minutes,
    plus chilling and freezing
Cooking time: 20 minutes

3 tablespoons Horlicks
450ml full fat milk
200ml double cream
1 vanilla pod
3 tablespoons malt extract
7 egg yolks
1 tablespoon soft light brown sugar
150g dark chocolate (70%),
    broken into chunks
a pinch of fine sea salt

ARMAGNAC ICE CREAM

This recipe came about when I was developing a new chocolate dessert and wanted an ice cream with a kick. The ice cream is silky smooth, with a punch of Armagnac.

Serve with double-baked chocolate mousse cake (see page 98).

Makes about 1 litre
Preparation time: 10 minutes,
    plus chilling and freezing
Cooking time: 20 minutes

250ml full fat milk
500ml double cream
8 egg yolks
185g caster sugar
200ml Armagnac

Pour the milk and cream into a heavy-based saucepan and bring to the boil.

Put your egg yolks and sugar into a large bowl and mix together. Once the milk is just boiling, pour it into the egg yolks, whisking constantly to prevent the eggs from curdling.

Pour back into the saucepan and cook the custard on a low heat, stirring all the time, until it can coat the back of a spoon. This will take approximately 10 minutes. Do not allow the custard to boil or you will end up with scrambled eggs.

Strain through a fine sieve, then whisk in the Armagnac and chill in an ice bath, made by filling a larger bowl one-third full with ice and water. Stir occasionally to stop a skin forming. When it's cold, lay a piece of clingfilm directly on the surface of the custard and place in the fridge until completely cold, or churn straight away in your ice cream machine. Churn according to the manufacturer's instructions, then transfer to a freezer-proof container and freeze until solid.

To make the ice cream by hand, take the mixture out of the freezer every 2–3 hours and give it a stir. Once it is softly set, beat it well with electric beaters, then freeze solid.

Great to serve with chocolate desserts, or just with a jug of hot chocolate sauce.

ALMOND ICE CREAM

The perfect thing about this ice cream is the way all the oils and flavour of the almonds really come through. It has an amazing flavour and is really smooth and velvety. Serve with chocolate terrine (see page 197), or on its own with raspberries.

Makes about 1 litre
Preparation time: 10 minutes, plus chilling and freezing
Cooking time: 20 minutes

200g flaked almonds
250ml full fat milk
500ml double cream
8 egg yolks
185g caster sugar

Preheat the oven to 180°C/fan 160°C/gas 4 and toast the flaked almonds for about 5–10 minutes, or until golden brown, turning them halfway through.

Meanwhile pour the milk and cream into a heavy-based saucepan and bring to the boil. Add the hot toasted almonds (adding them to the boiling milk will bring out the oils and flavour of the almonds) and simmer gently for 4 minutes.

Put the egg yolks and sugar into a large bowl and mix together. Pour the milk into the egg yolk mix, whisking constantly to prevent the eggs from curdling.

Pour back into the saucepan and cook the custard on a low heat, stirring all the time, until it can coat the back of a spoon. This will take approximately 10 minutes. Do not allow the custard to boil or you will end up with scrambled eggs.

Strain through a fine sieve and discard the almonds, then chill in an ice bath, made by filling a larger bowl one-third full with ice and water. Stir occasionally to stop a skin forming. When it's cold, lay a piece of clingfilm directly on the surface of the custard and place in the fridge until completely cold, or churn straight away in your ice cream machine. Churn according to the manufacturer's instructions, then transfer to a freezer-proof container and freeze until solid.

To make the ice cream by hand, take the mixture out of the freezer every 2–3 hours and give it a stir. Once it is softly set, beat it well with electric beaters, then freeze solid.

GOAT'S CHEESE ICE CREAM

I first made this ice cream a few years ago, for a large wedding party in the autumn. The couple wanted a cheese dessert but not cheesecake, and they also loved figs. It's quite unusual but it works really well, as it is still slightly sweet and has a slight savoury tang to it. Serve it with honey roast figs.

Pour the milk into a heavy-based saucepan and bring slowly to the boil. Put the egg yolks and sugar into a large bowl and mix together. When the milk is just boiling, pour it into the egg yolks, whisking constantly to prevent the eggs from curdling.

Pour back into the saucepan and cook the custard on a low heat, stirring all the time, until it can coat the back of a spoon. This will take approximately 10 minutes. Do not allow the custard to boil or you will end up with scrambled eggs.

Crumble in the goat's cheese and whisk until it has melted into the custard.

Strain through a fine sieve, then chill in an ice bath, made by filling a larger bowl one-third full with ice and water. Stir occasionally to stop a skin forming. When it's cold, lay a piece of clingfilm directly on the surface of the custard and place in the fridge until completely cold, or churn straight away in your ice cream machine. Churn according to the manufacturer's instructions, then transfer to a freezer-proof container and freeze until solid.

To make the ice cream by hand, take the mixture out of the freezer every 2–3 hours and give it a stir. Once it is softly set, beat it well with electric beaters, then freeze solid.

To make the honey roast figs, preheat the oven to 200°C/fan 180°C/gas 6. Cut a cross in the top of each fig about a quarter of the way down, then squeeze the bottom of the figs to make them bloom. Place the figs in a roasting tray and put a small knob of butter on top of each one, then drizzle over the honey and lemon juice. Bake for about 10 minutes, until the figs are soft and tender and the sauce is reduced.

Serve the figs with the goat's cheese ice cream and toasted brioche.

Makes about 1 litre
Preparation time: 10 minutes,
    plus chilling and freezing
Cooking time: 30 minutes

600ml full fat milk
5 egg yolks
80g caster sugar
220g soft goat's cheese
a pinch of fine sea salt

FOR THE HONEY
ROAST FIGS
2 or 3 figs per person
a knob of butter
1 tablespoon runny honey
juice of ½ a lemon

ISLESFORD DOCK SNOWBALLS

This recipe comes from a wonderful summer I spent in Maine, working with my wife Louise for the amazing Dan and Cynthia Lief at the Islesford Dock Restaurant on Little Cranberry Island. The Islesford Dock Restaurant is only open for about three months in the summer, but what they serve is amazing, fresh, local food – from the best crab cakes to my favourite, the 'Pearl Dog', and of course snowballs!

Serves 4 (2 balls per person)
Preparation time: 10 minutes,
   plus chilling and freezing
Cooking time: 5 minutes

Preheat the oven to 180°C/fan 160°C/gas 4 and line a baking tray with greaseproof paper.

Spread the desiccated coconut on a second baking tray and toast in the oven for about 5 minutes, stirring halfway through, until evenly golden brown. Stir in the salt and set aside to cool.

Allow the ice cream to soften slightly, then make 2 balls of vanilla ice cream per person. Place them on the prepared baking tray and put back into the freezer.

When ready to serve, take out the balls of ice cream, allow to soften for 5 minutes or so, then roll them in the coconut until all covered.

Serve immediately, with hot chocolate and caramel sauce.

Great to make with the kids. Yum!

100g desiccated coconut
a pinch of fine sea salt
1 batch of vanilla ice cream
   (see page 216)
1 batch of chocolate and caramel
   sauce (see page 248)

BUTTERMILK SORBET/SHERBET

This is a cross between a sorbet and a sherbet – it's very light and refreshing, and the vodka helps to give a smooth, scoopable finish. A bit of a grown-up dessert – really good served at the end of a meal.

Makes about 2 litres
Preparation time: 10 minutes,
    plus chilling and freezing
Cooking time: 30 minutes

250ml full fat milk
300ml double cream
1 vanilla pod
4 eggs
325g caster sugar
125ml glucose syrup
1 litre buttermilk
100ml vodka

Pour the milk and cream into a heavy-based saucepan. Split the vanilla pod lengthways and scrape out the seeds, then add both pod and seeds to the pan and bring the milk and cream slowly to the boil.

Put the eggs and sugar into a large bowl and mix together just for a minute, then pour the just-boiling cream over the mixture, whisking constantly. Place the bowl over a pan of simmering water and leave, whisking occasionally, until it reaches 80°C on a sugar thermometer (this takes about 20 minutes).

Take the bowl off the heat, add the glucose syrup and stir until dissolved. Stir in the buttermilk and vodka, then pass through a fine sieve into a plastic container (or jug/bowl), discarding the vanilla pod.

Chill quickly in an ice bath, made by filling a larger bowl one-third full with ice and water. Stir occasionally to stop a skin forming. When it's cold, lay a piece of clingfilm directly on the surface of the custard.

Refrigerate overnight, then churn in an ice cream machine according to the manufacturer's instructions. Transfer to a freezer-proof container and freeze until solid. To make the sorbet by hand, freeze the mix, taking it out of the freezer every 15–20 minutes to give it a stir.

Serve straight from the freezer.

BELLINI GRANITA

This recipe is my little twist on the classic cocktail. It makes a large amount, and is great served as a dessert in small glasses for big parties in the summer. Alternatively you can make it into your own cocktail by placing 3 or 4 tablespoons of the granita in a glass and adding some vodka and lemonade.

Makes about 2.4 litres
Preparation time: 20 minutes, plus chilling and freezing
Cooking time: 10 minutes

160g liquid glucose
10 very ripe peaches
juice of 2 lemons
350ml prosecco

FOR THE STOCK SYRUP
250g caster sugar
250ml water

First make the stock syrup. Put the sugar and water into a saucepan and bring to the boil, then reduce the heat and simmer for a couple of minutes, until a clear syrup is formed. Add the glucose and stir until dissolved.

Stone the peaches, then whiz them in a liquidizer with some of the stock syrup. Stir in the remaining stock syrup and pass the mixture through a fine sieve, then stir in the lemon juice and prosecco.

Pour into a metal dish and place in the freezer for about 30–40 minutes. As it begins to freeze, ice crystals will start to form around the edges. Scrape them into the centre, using a fork, then put back into the freezer and repeat until all is ice crystals and no juice is left.

Serve in beautiful frozen glasses or as a cocktail.

APPLE AND CIDER SORBET

I've made and served this sorbet in many of the restaurants I've worked in, always to good reviews. It uses lovely English Bramley apples and good cider. It's refreshing and cleans the palate after a big meal – it really hits the mark.

You can pour the mix directly into ice lolly moulds and freeze – great for summer.

Makes about 1.1 litres
Preparation time: 10 minutes,
    plus chilling and freezing
Cooking time: 30 minutes

Peel and core the apples and chop them into small pieces. Put them into a saucepan and add the cider, lemon zest, juice and sugar. Place on a medium heat and stir to dissolve the sugar, then bring to a light simmer and cook for about 20 minutes, or until the apple is soft.

Let the apple cool, then whiz in a food processor and strain through a fine sieve.

Put into the fridge until chilled, then churn according to the manufacturer's instructions. Transfer to a freezer-proof container and freeze until solid. To make the sorbet by hand, freeze the mix, taking it out of the freezer every 15–20 minutes to give it a stir.

Before serving, remove from the freezer and allow to soften for 5–10 minutes.

Great served with a shot of ice-cold vodka.

700g Bramley apples
500ml good-quality cider
zest and juice of 1 lemon
340g caster sugar

RASPBERRY SORBET

I make this sorbet a lot at home, as we are very lucky in having a few raspberry bushes in the garden. It has a really deep red fresh flavour but is quite sharp. Another good one to use in a sundae.

Whiz the raspberries in a food processor, then pass through a fine sieve into a bowl. Pour a quarter of the raspberry juice into a small saucepan and add the sugar and glucose, then place on a low heat until the sugar and glucose have dissolved. Pour into the rest of the raspberry juice.

Put into the fridge to chill, then churn according to the manufacturer's instructions. Transfer to a freezer-proof container and freeze until solid. To make the sorbet by hand, freeze the mix, taking it out of the freezer every 15–20 minutes to give it a stir.

To serve, remove from the freezer and allow to soften for 5–10 minutes.

Makes about 700g
Preparation time: 10 minutes, plus chilling and freezing
Cooking time: 5 minutes

750g raspberries
150g caster sugar
30ml liquid glucose

STRAWBERRY SORBET

The taste of summer – lovely served with a scoop of vanilla ice cream, like strawberries and cream. Keep an eye out for cheap strawberries through the summer, as you can use overripe ones for this, and a few bruised ones as well.

Makes about 1.2 litres
Preparation time: 10 minutes,
   plus chilling and freezing
Cooking time: 5 minutes

1kg fresh strawberries, hulled
165g caster sugar
200g liquid glucose
25g lemon juice

Whiz the strawberries in a food processor, then pass through a fine sieve into a bowl. Pour a quarter of the strawberry juice into a small saucepan and add the sugar and glucose, then place on a low heat until the sugar and glucose have melted. Pour into the rest of the strawberry juice and whisk in the lemon juice.

   Put into the fridge to chill, then churn according to the manufacturer's instructions. Transfer to a freezer-proof container and freeze until solid. To make the sorbet by hand, freeze the mix, taking it out of the freezer every 15–20 minutes to give it a stir.

   Remove from the freezer 5–10 minutes before serving.

THE STORE CUPBOARD

This chapter is very close to my heart, as I love to make pickles, jams and chutneys. It's nice to have a few things up your sleeve through the leaner months, and most of these recipes will keep happily for months and even improve with age. A spare jar of something can make a lovely gift too, if you can bear to give any away.

You can re-use old mayonnaise or olive jars – you don't have to buy new ones – but whatever type of jars you use, it is crucial to sterilize them properly when pickling or chutney- or jam-making. Here are some general notes and tips on how best to do it:

Heat the oven to 140°C/fan 120°C/gas 1. Wash the jars in hot soapy water and rinse thoroughly. Transfer to the oven (on a tray) and sterilize them for 20 minutes. Remove them carefully. Do not put cold foods into hot jars or hot foods into cold jars, otherwise the jars might shatter. Another more straightforward way of sterilizing jars is to run them through a hot cycle in the dishwasher, timing it so that the cycle ends when your jam or pickle or chutney is ready and still hot. It's best to let pickles/jams rest for about 15 minutes before potting.

Only use jar lids that are still in good condition and seal well on to the jar. The best jars for preserving are rubber-sealed ones like Kilner jars. It's best also to use wax seals and cellophane lids secured with a rubber band under the original lid. You can't sterilize the lid in the same way as the jars, so make sure they're super clean and even soak them in some sterilizer fluid if possible.

PRUNES IN ARMAGNAC

Use these plump and juicy prunes in prune, Armagnac and almond pudding (see page 164), or serve with chocolate desserts or honey mousse. They are also delicious on their own or with custard as a real treat.

Makes a 1.2 litre jar
Preparation time: 5 minutes
Standing time: minimum 2 months
  before use

625g pitted soft Agen prunes
about 500ml Armagnac

All you need to do is fill your jar up with prunes, cover them with Armagnac, put the lid on and leave for 2–3 months, turning the jar to mix the fruit up occasionally. Then they're ready to use.

The prunes will be used drained for most recipes, but the Armagnac soaking liquid can be kept and used for spooning over puddings and ice creams.

RAISINS IN RUM

Always ready for the rum and raisin ice cream, and also for the rum babas.

Makes a 1.2 litre jar
Preparation time: 5 minutes
Standing time: minimum 2 months
  before use

625g raisins
about 500ml dark rum

Just like the prunes in Armagnac – all you need to do is fill your jar up with raisins, cover them with dark rum, put the lid on and leave for 2–3 months, occasionally turning the jar to mix the fruit up. Then they're ready to use.

The raisins will be used drained for most recipes, but the dark rum soaking liquid can be kept and used for spooning over puddings and ice creams.

RASPBERRY JAM

Make sure you always have a few jars of raspberry jam – I try to make lots during the summer months, as I use it in a lot of recipes like jammy dodgers (see page 122) and Devonshire splits (see page 109).

Preheat the oven to 120°C/fan 100°C/gas ½.

Put the sugar into a roasting tin and warm it in the oven for about 25 minutes.

While the sugar is warming, put the raspberries and lemon juice into a preserving pan or large 8 litre pan and slowly, on a medium heat, bring to a light simmer. Once this point has been reached, turn down the heat to low and gradually stir in the sugar. Once the sugar has dissolved (which should happen quickly, as it is warm), bring to the boil and simmer until the setting point has been reached – this can take anything from 20 to 30 minutes, depending on how juicy your raspberries are.

Setting point: to test for the setting point, just take a teaspoon of jam and place it on a cold plate. Allow it to cool, then run your finger through it and if it doesn't run back on to itself, the setting point has been reached. Alternatively, once the jam is boiling, use a digital thermometer to measure the temperature until it reaches 104°C, when the setting point is reached.

Take the pan off the heat and leave for about 10 minutes, then whisk the foam on the top back into the jam and pour into warm sterilized jars.

Makes 1.2 kg
Preparation time: 5 minutes
Cooking time: 40 minutes

800g jam sugar
1kg raspberries
juice of 2 lemons

RHUBARB JAM

Ripple through some ice cream, or use as an alternative to raspberry jam in Devonshire splits (see page 109).

Makes 1.3kg
Preparation time: 15 minutes,
    plus overnight marinating
Cooking time: 25 minutes

1kg rhubarb
25g fresh ginger root
800g jam sugar
zest and juice of 1 orange

Prepare the rhubarb by trimming the top and bottom off each stalk and washing in cold water. Cut into 2cm chunks.

Peel the ginger and cut into very small dice.

Place the chopped rhubarb in a large bowl with the sugar, ginger, orange zest and juice. Mix well and leave overnight for about 10 hours – this will release the juices from the rhubarb.

Put the fruit and juices from the bowl into a large, heavy-based saucepan on a low heat and melt the sugar, stirring a few times. Once the sugar has dissolved, turn up the heat and bring to a rolling boil until the setting point is reached. Test as for the raspberry jam (see page 241), using a cold saucer; alternatively, using a digital thermometer when boiling, measure the temperature until it reaches 104°C, when the setting point is reached.

Pour the jam into warm sterilized jars.

SEVILLE ORANGE MARMALADE

First measure out the water into a bowl, then drop in the oranges and lemons and put into the fridge for 24 hours.

Remove the oranges and lemons and re-measure the water – it should be 2.15 litres, so if short, top it up.

Halve the oranges and lemons and squeeze the juice out, also scrape out all the pips, pith and pulp. Add the juice to the measured water. Put the pips, pith and pulp inside a piece of muslin, tie the top together, and add to the water as well.

Cut the juiced and scraped-out orange and lemon skins into thick strips and add to the water.

Pour the water, juice, muslin bag and strips of peel into a large, heavy-based saucepan or jam pan and bring to the boil. Then reduce the heat and simmer for 2 hours, until the peel is tender.

Now add all the sugar to the pan, stirring until it has dissolved. Turn up the heat and boil rapidly until the setting point is reached. Test as for the jams on the previous pages, using a cold saucer; alternatively, using a digital thermometer when boiling, measure the temperature until it reaches 104°C, when the setting point is reached.

Pour the marmalade into warm sterilized jars.

Makes about 4kg
Preparation time: 30 minutes,
    plus overnight marinating
Cooking time: about 3 hours

2.15 litres water
1kg Seville oranges
2 unwaxed lemons
900g granulated sugar
900g demerara sugar

LEMON CURD

I go direct in a saucepan, but if you feel more comfortable you can use a bowl over simmering water, which will give you more control (if you don't have direct heat under the saucepan it won't cook as fast).

Use in lemon meringue ice cream (see page 220), and it's also great on toast or in a doughnut.

For blood orange curd, replace 4 of the lemons with 4 blood oranges. Don't zest the lemons, but zest 3 of the blood oranges instead.

Zest 2 of the lemons and juice all 6. Place the zest and juice in a large saucepan, add the butter and sugar, and melt together on a low heat, stirring to ensure all the sugar dissolves. Once melted and not too hot, add the beaten eggs, whisking all the time.

Cook over a fairly low heat, whisking constantly, until thick and glossy (about 3 minutes), then pass through a fine sieve and pour into warm sterilized jars.

Makes 1 kg
Preparation time: 20 minutes
Cooking time: 10 minutes

6 large lemons
200g unsalted butter, cubed
400g granulated sugar
6 eggs, beaten

BUTTERSCOTCH CRUNCH

Ready to use for ice cream, and lovely to use as a sprinkle over desserts or just to suck on as a sweet.

Line a large baking tray with non-stick baking paper.

Pour the water into a heavy-based saucepan and bring to the boil, then turn down the heat to low and add the sugar and butter. Let them slowly melt, stirring gently, and once the sugar has dissolved and the butter has melted, turn the heat up and bring back to a simmer until it turns a golden brown and reaches a temperature of 120–123°C (about 25 minutes). Pour on to the prepared baking tray – watch out, as it's very hot – and leave to cool completely and set hard.

Crack the butterscotch crunch into small and different shaped shards with a rolling pin, and place in a large jar. Keeps for a few weeks.

Makes 400g
Preparation time: 5 minutes
Cooking time: 35 minutes

140ml water
500g caster sugar
60g unsalted butter, cubed

HONEYCOMB

There are one million and one uses for honeycomb: rippled through ice cream, sprinkled over doughnuts or trifles, and served with creamy desserts for a bit of crunch.

Makes 350g
Preparation time: 5 minutes
Cooking time: 15 minutes

Line a large baking tray with baking paper.

Put the honey, glucose, sugar and water into a saucepan and bring to the boil, stirring a little to dissolve the sugar, then reduce the heat and simmer until a light brown caramel is reached (about 10 minutes). Turn off the heat and whisk in the sifted bicarbonate of soda for 5 seconds. Watch out, as it will fizz and bubble straight away. Pour on to your prepared tray and leave to cool completely and harden.

When cold, break into small pieces and store in an airtight container.

40g pure clear honey
70ml liquid glucose
200g caster sugar
2½ tablespoons water
1 tablespoon bicarbonate
   of soda, sifted

HAZELNUT (OR ANY NUT) PRALINE

Ready for ice cream, and great for sprinkling on doughnuts and desserts.

Makes 500g
Preparation time: 10 minutes
Cooking time: 35 minutes

375g blanched hazelnuts
225g caster sugar

Preheat the oven to 180°C/ fan 160°C /gas 4 and lightly oil a baking tray.

Put the hazelnuts on a second baking tray and toast them in the oven for about 20 minutes, or until golden brown, checking them halfway through.

Put the sugar into a heavy-based saucepan and melt it on a low heat for 3–4 minutes, then turn up the heat and let it become a dark brown caramel. Take off the heat and add the hazelnuts. Stir, then pour out on to your prepared tray and leave to cool. While the nuts are cooling, clean your saucepan by filling the pan up with water and bringing it to a light simmer until all the caramel has melted into the water.

Once the hazelnut praline is cold and hard, break it into small pieces with a rolling pin. Then whiz it to fine crumbs in a food processor.

Store in an airtight container.

CHOCOLATE AND CARAMEL SAUCE

Serve with ice cream or 'crunch in the mouth' (page 210). Will keep for a month or two in a sterilized jar.

Makes 800g
Preparation time: 5 minutes
Cooking time: 20 minutes

310g caster sugar
300g dark chocolate (70%), chopped
375ml double cream

Put the sugar into a large, heavy-based saucepan and melt over a medium heat, stirring occasionally, letting it turn into a dark brown caramel (but not burnt). Once you have the right colour, stop the caramel going any further by adding the chocolate, then the cream. Stir together – the caramel will go all stringy but don't worry, as you heat it through it will dissolve into a smooth chocolate sauce.

Heat the sauce through, occasionally whisking it with a balloon whisk to smooth it out. Once you have heated the chocolate mix on a low heat until it is all dissolved into a sauce (this takes 3 – 4 minutes over a low heat), pass it through a fine sieve and pour it into warm sterilized jars.

GOAT'S MILK CARAMEL

This is a simply delicious caramel – the goat's milk gives it a slight tangy taste and it's great simply spooned over vanilla ice cream.

Makes 500g
Preparation time: 5 minutes
Cooking time: 1 hour

1 litre whole goat's milk
375g granulated sugar
¼ teaspoon bicarbonate of soda
1 bay leaf
¼ teaspoon vanilla extract

Pour half the goat's milk into a large, heavy based saucepan and add the sugar. Bring to the boil, stirring to dissolve the sugar, then simmer vigorously, whisking occasionally with a balloon whisk for about 20–25 minutes, or until it goes a light golden brown. Remove from the heat.

Put the rest of the goat's milk into a separate saucepan and add the bicarbonate of soda, bay leaf and vanilla extract. Bring to the boil, then slowly and very carefully add it to the caramel mix – it will fizz up the side of the saucepan and bubble furiously. Make sure you stir constantly once all the milk has gone in, and bring back to a simmer until a smooth caramel is reached, whisking frequently with a balloon whisk (the temperature on a thermometer should be 110–112°C). Strain through a sieve, discarding the bay leaf, and pour into warm sterilized jars. Leave to cool.

Serve at room temperature or slightly heated, with ice cream.

MERINGUES

This recipe works but you need to weigh your egg whites. You can buy fresh egg whites in cartons in most supermarkets now, which are ideal for this recipe, but if you make ice cream you will always have egg whites left over (they freeze really well).

Preheat the oven to 140°C/fan 120°C/gas 1 and line a large baking tray with non-stick baking paper.

Using an electric mixer with a whisk attachment, whisk the egg whites stiffly on high speed for 3 minutes, then turn down to a low speed and add all the sugar in one go. Turn back to a high speed and whisk until thick, stiff and glossy (about 8 minutes).

Make mounds of the meringue on your prepared baking tray, using a large spoon or a piping bag with a wide plain nozzle.

Bake for about 1 hour, then remove from the tray (they will lift off easily) and put on a rack to cool.

Makes 8
Preparation time: 15 minutes
Cooking time: 1 hour

120g egg whites (roughly 4 large egg whites)
240g caster sugar

PUMPKIN SEED OIL

This is used for the pumpkin seed bread in the baking chapter (see page 36), but it is also very useful for drizzling over salads or roasted vegetables.

Makes 300ml
Preparation time: 10 minutes
Cooking time: 5 minutes
Standing time: 1 month

300ml sunflower oil
100g pumpkin seeds

Put the oil into a saucepan and warm very gently.

Toast the pumpkin seeds in a large frying pan on a low heat – keep tossing them so they don't burn – until speckled light brown and starting to pop.

While the pumpkin seeds are still warm, crush them in a pestle and mortar to release their flavours. Put them into a warm sterilized jar and pour over your warm oil, then cover and leave for at least 1 month.

TOMATO AND CHILLI CHUTNEY

Great with sweet onion and fine herb tart (see page 73), in a ham and cheese sandwich, or as a dip for crudités. If you leave it a few weeks before using, it will develop an even better depth of flavour.

Makes 400g
Preparation time: 15 minutes
Cooking time: 2 hours

Cut the tomatoes into quarters and the green chilli into small pieces (leave the seeds in). Finely dice the onion and crush the garlic.

Put the tomatoes, chilli, onion and garlic into a large, heavy-based saucepan, add the rest of the ingredients and slowly bring to the boil. Once boiling, turn down to a light simmer and cook uncovered for about 1½–2 hours, or until the ingredients are soft and you have a thick paste left. If you can find them, take out the bay leaves and rosemary sprig and throw them away, as they have done their job.

Pour into warm sterilized jars.

The chutney is ready to eat pretty much straight away, but best if you leave it for a few weeks to settle. Once opened, best kept in the fridge.

5 large ripe tomatoes
1 long green chilli
1 onion
4 cloves of garlic
1 teaspoon fine sea salt
1 teaspoon paprika
1 teaspoon chilli powder
1 teaspoon black mustard seeds
25g demerara sugar
25g caster sugar
300ml white wine vinegar
2 bay leaves
a 12cm sprig of fresh rosemary
¼ teaspoon ground allspice

PICCALILLI

This piccalilli is full of flavour and packed with vegetables that have a delightful crunch. The recipe makes a lot, but it keeps very well for a year and trust me, it won't last long once opened. Make sure you always keep a few jars for Christmas – and so you can give a few away as presents.

Makes 4 kg
Preparation time: 40 minutes,
    plus soaking time
Cooking time: 15 minutes

Cut the cauliflowers into small florets and place them in a large bowl. Sprinkle with 45g of the sea salt and toss, then cover the bowl and put into the fridge for 24 hours.

Rinse the cauliflower for about 15 minutes under a running cold tap, then leave to drain.

Peel the onions and cut them into bite-size pieces, about 1cm, then deseed the cucumbers and dice in the same way as the onions. Place the onions and cucumbers in a large bowl and sprinkle with the remainder of the sea salt. Again toss the vegetables in the salt, then cover the bowl and leave for 50 minutes.

Rinse the cucumber and onions for about 10 minutes and leave to drain.

Put both vinegars, the chillies and the bay leaf into a large saucepan or preserving pan (big enough to hold all the ingredients), and bring to the boil, then reduce the heat and simmer for 5 minutes. Meanwhile mix the sugar, mustard powder, turmeric and cornflour in a bowl and put to one side.

Leave the vinegar to cool a little, then take out the chillies and bay leaf. Then leave it to cool completely.

Once the vinegar is cold, whisk in the mustard mix. Bring back to the boil, then simmer rapidly for about 4–5 minutes, whisking fairly constantly to prevent it sticking to the bottom of the pan. It should be nice and thick now. Turn off the heat and add the cauliflower florets, diced onion and cucumber. Mix well and place in warm sterilized jars.

You can eat this straight away, but it's even better if you leave it for a week or so to settle. Happy days.

2 medium cauliflowers
65g fine sea salt
4 large onions
2 cucumbers
1.2 litres white wine vinegar
500ml malt vinegar
4 dried bird's-eye chillies
1 bay leaf
725g caster sugar
110g mustard powder
40g ground turmeric
7 tablespoons cornflour

PLUM KETCHUP

This is a slightly different twist on the traditional tomato version, but it has more piquancy and works really well with bacon and corn munchies (see page 76) or in a BLT or a turkey and stuffing sandwich.

Makes 1.5 litres
Preparation time: 20 minutes
Cooking time: 1 hour 10 minutes

Put all the ingredients into a really large heavy-based saucepan or preserving pan and cook on a low heat, stirring occasionally, until the plums have softened. Turn up the heat to medium for about 20–25 minutes, then back down to a low heat for another 20–25 minutes. Remove the bay leaves and the orange and lemon strips, and continue to cook until it thickens up a little (turning the heat up slightly if you need to). You will need to keep an eye on it, as it can catch and burn on the bottom, so stir often.

Leave the ketchup to cool for 10 minutes, then whiz it up with a stick blender – you can leave it chunky or whiz until smooth, it's up to you.

Pour into a warm sterilized bottle or jars, and leave for about 2 weeks before using. Refrigerate once opened.

1.5kg plums, stoned and halved
4 small onions, peeled and
    roughly chopped
4 cloves of garlic, peeled and
    crushed
500ml white wine vinegar
25g fine sea salt
225g demerara sugar
1 hot green chilli, chopped
    (seeds left in)
2 bay leaves
1 strip of lemon rind
1 strip of orange rind

PICKLED ONIONS

No store cupboard would be complete without these. Great with cheese and crackers.

Peel the onions (put them into a bowl, pour boiling water over them and leave for a few minutes, then drain and cool; the skins should come off easily). Put the peeled onions into a large bowl and sprinkle with the salt, then cover with clingfilm and leave at room temperature for 24 hours (tossing two or three times).

Rinse the onions under cold running water for 30 minutes, then drain and place in three 2 litre jars. Fill up two of the jars with malt vinegar and one with white wine vinegar, then strain the vinegar from the jars into a saucepan. Add another 500ml of white wine vinegar and add the rest of the ingredients. Bring to a fast boil, then reduce the heat and simmer for 20 minutes. Meanwhile, take the onions out of the jars and sterilize the jars.

Once the jars are ready, pop the onions back in. Strain the vinegar over them while still warm, and seal. Leave for 1 month to settle and, once opened, store in the fridge.

Makes 4 litres
Preparation time: 45 minutes,
    plus salting time
Cooking time: 25 minutes

2kg pickling onions
110g sea salt
1 litre malt vinegar
1 litre white wine vinegar
2 bay leaves
1 teaspoon yellow mustard seeds
2 bird's-eye chillies
1 teaspoon black peppercorns
2 tablespoons demerara sugar
12 allspice berries
1 star anise
12–14 juniper berries
20 coriander seeds
1 teaspoon fennel seeds
2 mace blades

PICKLED TOMATOES

Perfect with truffle, cheese and potato pie (see page 62), but also lovely with grilled fish.

Makes one 500g jar
Preparation time: 10 minutes
Cooking time: 10 minutes

Get a small knife and prick each tomato several times, then pop them into a sterilized 500g jar.

Put the rest of the ingredients into a saucepan and bring to the boil, then reduce the heat and simmer for 2–3 minutes, making sure all the sugar has dissolved. Take the pan off the heat and leave for 2 minutes.

Pour the mixture – with all the flavourings still in – over the tomatoes and seal the jar. The tomatoes keep unopened for about 6 months. Store in the fridge once opened.

550g tomatoes (about
   35 cherry tomatoes)
600ml white wine vinegar
2 bay leaves
½ teaspoon black peppercorns
½ teaspoon yellow mustard seeds
¼ teaspoon fine sea salt
80g demerara sugar
2 bird's-eye chillies
½ teaspoon fennel seeds
2 or 3 sprigs of fresh thyme

PICKLED GARLIC

Makes one small jar (but it goes a long way). I love to slice this over Gellatly pizza (see page 83). You can also use it in risotto and pasta dishes, or pop a few cloves into a braise.

Peel all the garlic cloves and put them into a saucepan with all the other ingredients. Bring slowly to the boil, then reduce the heat and simmer for 2 minutes. Transfer to a warm sterilized jar.

Makes one 500g jar
Preparation time: 15 minutes
Cooking time: 10 minutes

4 bulbs of garlic
150ml white wine vinegar
2 tablespoons caster sugar
1 tablespoon fine sea salt
2 bird's-eye chillies
1 bay leaf
2 sprigs of fresh thyme

PICKLED BEETROOT

Lovely with Otter Camp pasties (see page 74), and also great with cheese or with sweet onion and fine herb tart (see page 73).

Makes 800g
Preparation time: 5 minutes
Cooking time: 1½ hours

Trim the raw beetroots and place them in a large saucepan. Fill up the pan with water, bring to the boil, then reduce the heat and simmer partially covered for 1¼–1½ hours, until a small sharp knife goes into the beetroots easily. Leave to cool completely in the water, then drain and slip off the skins.

Cut the cooked beetroot into medium chunks and mix with the diced onion. Put into a large saucepan along with the other ingredients and bring to the boil, then remove the pan from the heat.

Spoon the beetroot and onion into warm sterilized jars, then pour over the vinegar and seal.

Leave for 1 month to settle. Will keep for a good year. Once opened, store in the fridge.

600g raw beetroots (about 4 large beetroots)
1 large onion, peeled and diced small
1 teaspoon ground ginger
¼ teaspoon smoked paprika
4 dried bird's-eye chillies
1 bay leaf
1 sprig of fresh rosemary
450ml white wine vinegar
20g demerara sugar

BREAD AND BUTTER PICKLES

These are the Rolls Royce of pickles – fantastic in a burger, a steak sandwich or just on some toasted sourdough.

Cut the baby cucumbers into slices about 1cm thick and put them into a bowl with the sliced onions. Sprinkle with the sea salt and mix together. Leave for 12 hours.

Leaving the cucumbers and onions in the bowl, rinse thoroughly under cold running water for 15 minutes, emptying the bowl of water every 10 minutes, then drain.

Place all the other ingredients in a large saucepan and bring to the boil, then reduce the heat and simmer for 5 minutes, making sure all the sugar has dissolved. Pour, while still hot, into the bowl of drained cucumbers and onions and leave to stand for 5 minutes.

Put into warm sterilized jars, where it will keep for 6 months.

Makes 2.5kg (but after you have tasted these pickles you will want to double the recipe)
Preparation time: 50 minutes, plus salting time
Cooking time: 10 minutes

2.7kg baby cucumbers
1kg onions, peeled and sliced
125g sea salt
1 litre cider vinegar
1.1kg caster sugar
3 tablespoons mustard seeds
3 tablespoons cumin seeds
1½ teaspoons ground turmeric
1½ teaspoons cayenne pepper

LIST OF STOCKISTS

FLOUR

There is a lot of good flour available to buy in supermarkets, for example:

Doves Farm flour
(also from www.dovesfarm.co.uk)

Allinson flour
(from all major supermarkets)

There is also a lot of great flour you can get online, such as:

Cann Mill flour
(www.stoatesflour.co.uk)

Marriage's, which we use at the bakery Bread Ahead (www.flour.co.uk)

YEAST

Kronjast Farsk Jast (www.ocado.com)

EQUIPMENT

For mixers, proving baskets, tins, trays, baking stones and anything else you might need:

www.bakerybits.co.uk

www.kitchenaid.co.uk

www.lakeland.co.uk

www.kenwoodworld.com/uk

www.nisbets.co.uk

www.johnlewis.com

ACKNOWLEDGEMENTS

First I would like to thank Juliet Annan and Sophie Missing for all their encouragement and support for my book – you are both wonderful.

To Andy Sewell for the amazing photos and Andy Knowles for the rock 'n' roll baking videos – you are both geniuses.

To Nathan Burton for the design, Annie Lee for copy-editing, Bren Parkins-Knight and Jan Stevens for recipe testing, and Ellie Smith, James Blackman, Julia Murday, and everyone else at Penguin who has worked on the book.

To Philip Crowther, Peter Harrison, Paul Merrett and Fergus Henderson for showing me the ways of the Jedi.

To Margot Henderson for the amazing cooking journeys and the many wise words.

To Luka Mokliak for being a great friend and an amazing baker.

To Allan Jenkins and the Gentle Author for all your support over the years.

To Matt Jones for trusting in me and Louise.

To Dave, Katie, Stu and Lucy for support and friendship.

To Planet Rock for keeping me rocking in the bakery.

To Maya and Luke for giving us the light.

To my Saturday girls, Katie, Georgia and Lucy Duncan for all being amazing.

To Karl Goward, Tom Pemberton, James Lowe, Chris Gillard, Lillie O'Brien, Abbey Dempsey, A-Cau, Kitty Travers, Edd Lewis, Therese Gustafsson, Tom Harris, Ben Lindsay, Lee Tiernan, Eric Cooper, Dan and Cynthia Leif, Tom Blythe, Jason Lowe, Jonathon Jones, James Ferguson, Susan Cowie, Randolph Hodgson, Tif Hunter, Clerkenwell boy, Fabio Ferreira, Nichola Gensler.

And thanks to all the great people I have worked with.

INDEX

Page references for photographs are in **bold**